Inspire English International

Year 7 Workbook

T0346009

Ben Hulme-Cross

Contents

Contents

About the Workbook

Welcome to Inspire English International! We hope you will find this book useful (and inspiring!) as you develop your skill and knowledge in written English. Through explicitly addressing the areas needed to excel in English you should gain mastery of the subject and make excellent progress.

The books have been written using a mix of real-world texts and purpose-written passages, designed to inspire discussion and help to maintain a focus on key curriculum objectives.

This Workbook gives you the chance to practise and embed the key skills introduced in the Student Book and through teaching, thereby deepening and broadening your understanding. Clear links are provided between this book and the Student Book and daily teaching, to support this further.

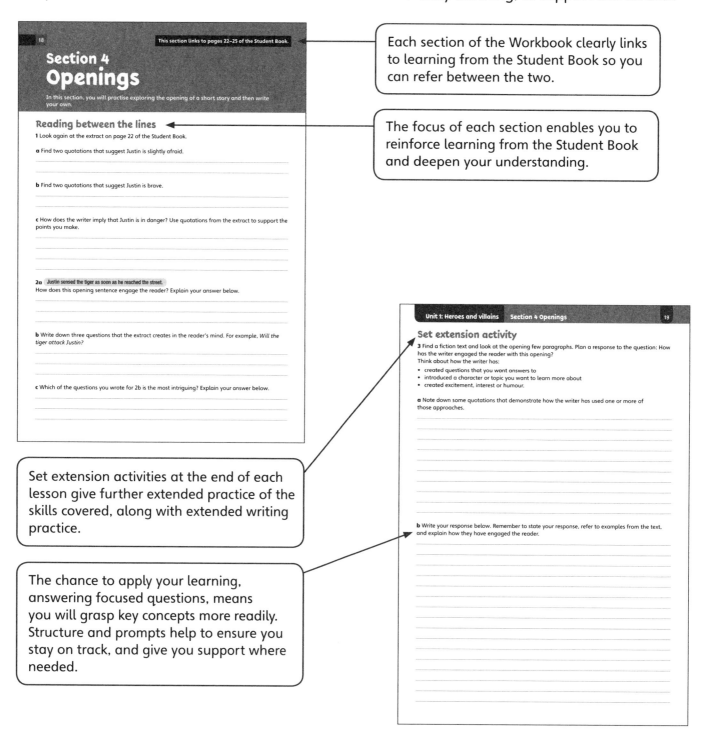

Each section of the Workbook clearly links to learning from the Student Book so you can refer between the two.

The focus of each section enables you to reinforce learning from the Student Book and deepen your understanding.

Set extension activities at the end of each lesson give further extended practice of the skills covered, along with extended writing practice.

The chance to apply your learning, answering focused questions, means you will grasp key concepts more readily. Structure and prompts help to ensure you stay on track, and give you support where needed.

About the Workbook

Innovative assessment sections explain clearly how to proofread and improve a response, and then give you the chance to put your learning into practice.

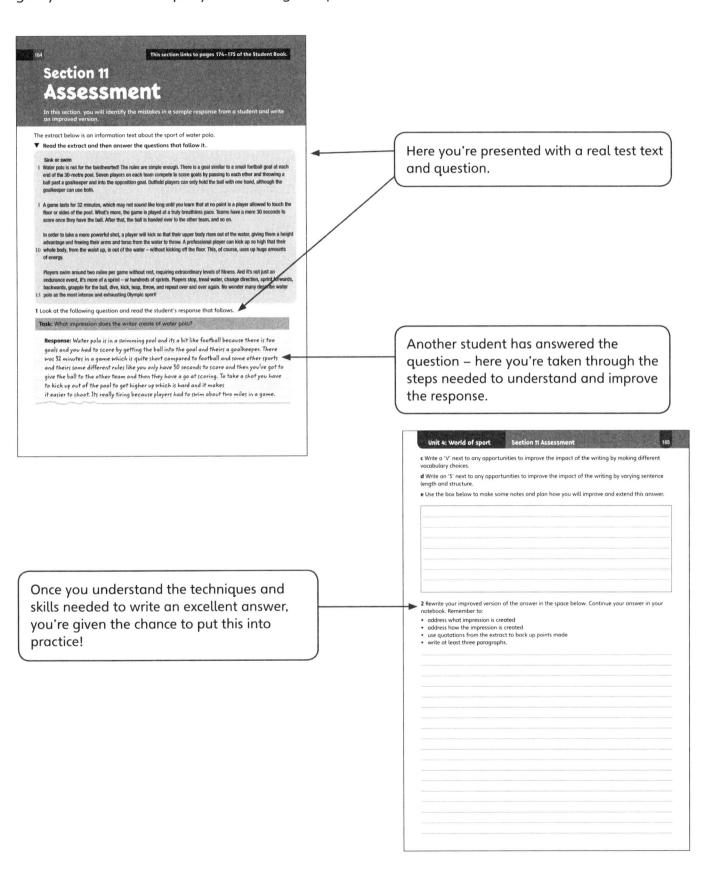

Here you're presented with a real test text and question.

Another student has answered the question – here you're taken through the steps needed to understand and improve the response.

Once you understand the techniques and skills needed to write an excellent answer, you're given the chance to put this into practice!

This section links to pages 10–13 of the Student Book.

Section 1
Description

In this section, you will practise exploring key ideas and vocabulary choices the writer has used to create an engaging description.

Comprehension

1 Read the extract on page 10 of the Student Book. Place the things that the narrator hears, does and experiences below in the order that they appear in the extract. Number each point from 1 to 5.

A She cups her hands over her mouth ☐   **B** Her Mum shouts a warning ☐

C She hears a deafening noise ☐   **D** She is thrown against a rock ☐

E She hears a shout ☐

Inference

2 Read this quotation from the extract:

My skis were off, and I was tumbling helplessly forwards into the snow. My terror grew in a flash as I remembered the huge drop that lay nearby. Would I be hurled into a chasm? Or would I be buried under metres of snow and suffocate? Which was worse?

a Tick any of the following emotions that suggest how the narrator is feeling in the quotation above.

A helpless ☐   **B** excited ☐   **C** scared ☐   **D** angry ☐   **E** thrilled ☐

b Write a sentence explaining each choice.

_____

_____

_____

_____

3a Look again at the extract on page 10 of the Student Book. Make a list of all the words and phrases you can find that suggest the character has some hope.

_____

_____

_____

b Now identify the first moment where it seems the narrator feels hopeful. Write a sentence or two explaining your choice.

_____

_____

_____

Set extension activity

4 Think of five feelings or emotions. Write one in each of the boxes below. For each one, add at least five descriptive words or phrases that would describe someone experiencing those feelings. An example is provided.

Emotion	fear
Description	cold
	trembling
	shaking
	heart beating
	sweating

Emotion	
Description	

Emotion	
Description	

Emotion	
Description	

Emotion	
Description	

Emotion	
Description	

Vocabulary choices

5a Look again at the third paragraph of the extract on page 10 of the Student Book. Write down three words or phrases the writer uses to suggest the narrator feels she is helpless.

_____

_____

_____

b Using your response to **Activity 5a**, write a sentence explaining how the writer's vocabulary choices create the sense of helplessness.

_____

_____

Sentence punctuation

6 Check the punctuation of the following sentences. Place a tick next to those that are correct. Place a cross next to any that are incorrect. Circle the errors.

A What a brilliant party!   ☐

B is Manchester the best city in England?   ☐

C Last night I couldn't sleep   ☐

D She was shaking with laughter.   ☐

E That video is cool?   ☐

Writing descriptions

7 Imagine a situation in which you are looking out from a hiding place. It could be part of a game, you could be spying on someone, or maybe you are hiding from something dangerous.

a In one word, describe the atmosphere of the situation. For example: _funny, scary._

_____

b Using precise vocabulary, name two things you can see in your imagined situation that help create the atmosphere you mentioned in **Activity 7a**. Add descriptive words to create a clear picture, completing the table below. An example is provided.

What can you see?	Descriptive words
my brother	sneaky, clumsy, heavy, sweaty, whistling, unaware, stomping, snoring

c Write a sentence describing one of the things you listed in the table above. Think about the atmosphere you want to create, and choose only the most suitable descriptive words.

_____

_____

Set extension activity

8a Add two more paragraphs to the description that you began in **Activity 7** on the previous page. Answers should use carefully chosen language to:

- describe what is happening in the situation (for example, why it is funny or scary)
- describe the character's reaction to the situation
- create the right atmosphere using descriptive language.

b Look back at your writing and correct any mistakes, paying particular attention to punctuation.

c Highlight or underline any words you have used that are particularly effective in creating the atmosphere or showing the character's feelings.

This section links to pages 14–17 of the Student Book.

Section 2
Information

In this section, you will practise identifying and summarising key points, exploring how the writer has structured them.

Key points

1 Look at these five quotations taken from the first three paragraphs of the informative article 'Getting lost in the desert' on page 14 of the Student Book. Place a tick next to the quotation that makes the key point.

A you will certainly need to make some important decisions to stay alive ☐

B your number one priority is to look for ways to reduce your exposure ☐

C there are three key things to remember ☐

D The desert heat will make you very thirsty ☐

2a Reread the third section of the text: **Get help.** Write down three key points that are made in this section.

_____

_____

_____

b Which of the three points you have listed is the most important? Write a sentence explaining your answer.

_____

_____

Summaries

3 Read the following summaries of the second section of the text: **Drink water.** Which do you think is the most effective summary? Write a sentence explaining your choice.

A You will be very thirsty, but do not drink all your water at once.

B Sip your water slowly to avoid dehydration. Drink a little more if you feel dizzy. Eat in small amounts.

C Eat and drink in small amounts.

_____

_____

4 Write your own summary of the whole article in at least three sentences. Aim to write 40 to 60 words.

_____

_____

Set extension activity

5a Identify a topic you are interested in. For example: a sport, a hobby, an important issue in the world or a historical event.

b Imagine you have been asked to write an informative article about your chosen topic. Write down five key points that you would make in this article.

Key points	Order

c Now think about the best order in which to make the points. Write the numbers 1–5 in the 'Order' column of the table to indicate which point should come first, second, etc.

d Write a paragraph summarising the article you would write. Your summary should include each of the five points that you listed in the table.

12

Structure

6 Draw lines linking each of these structural features to the sentence explaining its purpose.

Structural feature	Purpose
Heading	Gives a short overview of the issue or topic
Introduction	Identifies the topics covered by each section of text
Subheadings	Provides detailed information
Text under subheadings	Identifies the subject of the article

7 Look at the following statements about the order in which writers choose to make their points. Which of the statements are true and which are false? Circle T or F for each statement.

A A good writer may put the most important point first to emphasise its importance.   [T / F]

B A good writer may organise the points by looking at how much space each will take up.   [T / F]

C A good writer may choose to put the most important point last to finish the article in a very persuasive way.   [T / F]

D A good writer may decide that it does not matter how the points are ordered.   [T / F]

Adverbials of time

8 Look at the list of words below. Place a tick next to each word that is an adverbial of time.

Finally	☐	Never	☐
Firstly	☐	Summary	☐
Furthermore	☐	Surprisingly	☐
However	☐	There	☐
Lastly	☐	Thirdly	☐

9 Look at these three points taken from the first section of the extract on page 14 of the Student Book: **Keep covered**. Write a paragraph of text including all three points, beginning each sentence with an adverbial of time.

A Look for ways to reduce your exposure.

B Cover your head to protect against direct sun.

C Keep yourself as warm as possible at night.

_____

_____

_____

_____

_____

Set extension activity

10 In **Activity 5** on page 11 of this Workbook, you wrote a summary of an article on a topic of your choice. You are now going to write the article. Use the template below to help structure your ideas. Make sure that you include:

- a heading
- an introduction
- two or three subheadings
- text under the subheadings
- ideas linked by adverbials of time.

Heading: _____

Introduction

_____

_____

_____

_____

Subheading: _____

_____

_____

_____

_____

_____

_____

Subheading: _____

_____

_____

_____

_____

_____

_____

_____

Subheading: _____

_____

_____

_____

_____

This section links to pages 18–21 of the Student Book.

Section 3
Intention and response

In this section, you will practise considering the writer's intention and your response, supporting it with evidence from the text.

Writers' intentions

1 Read the extract on page 18 of the Student Book. What does the writer want us to feel about the characters and their situation? Write one or two sentences below.

_____

_____

_____

_____

Finding evidence

2 Find quotations from the extract to use as evidence for each of the following statements.

The writer wants us to sense the danger before the characters do.
Evidence:

There is a brief moment of hope towards the end of the extract.
Evidence:

Responding to the text

3 Write a short paragraph answering the following question, using quotations from the extract to support your answer: Which section in the extract creates the highest sense of tension? Remember to add speech marks around the quotations.

_____

_____

_____

_____

_____

_____

Set extension activity

4a You are now going to write two paragraphs responding to a text (either part of a novel or an article) you have recently read and enjoyed.

Make brief notes answering each of the following questions.

(i) | How did the writer want the reader to feel?

(ii) | What did the writing make you feel?

(iii) | How did the writer make you feel as you did?

b Use the notes you have made to write two paragraphs responding to the text you have chosen. Include quotations from the text. Continue your answer in your notebook if needed.

New paragraphs

5 Look at the text below. It should be split into two paragraphs. Mark the place where the text should be split, then explain your choice in the space provided.

It took us about half an hour to get all our things into the car. Not that Tom did anything, of course. He just sang his stupid song and banged his dinosaur against the car window while Dad and Mum and I ran around trying to get everything ready. It was going to be a long drive to the airport! By the time we got there, Dad was in a rage.

Structuring the text

6a Look at the extract on page 18 of the Student Book from when the storm hits. Complete the following sentences.

There is a moment of hope when _____

_____

Then the situation worsens when _____

_____

Finally, the situation gets better when _____

_____

b The mood goes from hope to despair and back to hope again. Why has the writer chosen to structure the text in this way? Write one or two sentences explaining your view.

_____

_____

_____

7 Imagine you are travelling somewhere by boat, on your own. Various things happen on your journey, some of which make you feel unsafe. Look at this list of events.

A It begins to hail   **F** You have something to eat

B You notice a small leak in the boat   **G** Your engine fails

C Storm clouds gather overhead   **H** It is a mild spring day

D Your water bottle breaks   **I** Something big crashes into the bottom of the boat

E Your bag falls out of the boat and sinks   **J** You repair the leak

Reorder the list of events so that the sense of danger builds towards a moment of greatest tension at the end. Intersperse the moments that feel safer.

A _____   **F** _____

B _____   **G** _____

C _____   **H** _____

D _____   **I** _____

E _____   **J** _____

Set extension activity

8 Plan two different ways in which you could continue the story from **Activity 7**, achieving different intentions. For example, you could create a sense of mystery, adventure and excitement, or create sympathy for the narrator. Before you begin each plan, ask yourself:

- What feeling am I trying to create (for example, *tension*, *sympathy*)?
- What happens to the character?
- How does the character feel or respond?
- How will I order events to achieve my intended effect?

Plan 1

Plan 2

9 Now select the plan that you feel has the most interesting structure and effects. Explain why you chose this plan.

This section links to pages 22–25 of the Student Book.

Section 4
Sentence structure for effect

In this section, you will practise exploring how writers use sentence length to express their ideas and to help them to achieve their intention.

Identifying the writer's intention

1 The writer uses words to present Mira and the bear in a certain way. Find a quotation from the extract on page 22 of the Student Book to support each of the following statements.

a Mira is excited.

_____

b Mira is curious.

_____

c The bear is wild.

_____

d Mira is scared.

_____

e Mira is brave.

_____

f The bear calms down.

_____

The effect of sentence structures

2 The writer uses short sentences in the seventh paragraph. What atmosphere does this help the writer to create? Write a sentence explaining your view.

_____

_____

3 Look again at the first paragraph. How do the length and rhythm of the sentences reflect Mira's thoughts and feelings? Write a paragraph explaining your answer.

_____

_____

_____

_____

_____

Set extension activity

4 For each of the grammatical terms in the boxes below, find at least three examples in the extract on page 22 of the Student Book. Then write a definition of each term.

Noun
Examples
1
2
3
Definition

Clause
Examples
1
2
3
Definition

Verb
Examples
1
2
3
Definition

Conjunction
Examples
1
2
3
Definition

Conjunctions

5 Underline the conjunction in each of the following sentences.

a I ran for the bus so I wouldn't be late.

b He swam more slowly because he wanted to save his energy.

c She decided to keep going until it was dark.

d I said yes although I wasn't happy about it.

e The cat purred and she went to sit in the sun.

6 How many clauses are there in each of these sentences? Write the number of clauses next to each sentence.

a I ran because I was terrified.   _____

b I fell backwards.   _____

c When I heard the car I panicked, and then everything went wrong.   _____

Varying sentence length

7a Imagine a scene in which a character is in danger. Make a few notes outlining what happens in the scene and how the character feels.

_____

_____

_____

_____

b Write a short scene in which your character is in danger and beginning to panic. Use only short sentences as the danger and panic increase.

_____

_____

_____

_____

_____

_____

c Describe the moment in which the danger becomes less immediate. Describe the character's thoughts and feelings, using a mixture of short and longer, multi-clause sentences.

_____

_____

_____

_____

_____

Set extension activity

8 Revise the skills you have covered in the first half of this unit, ready for the assessment in the next lesson. You may find it helpful to note down the key points covered in each of the sections so far. If there are any areas where you do not feel confident, reread the appropriate pages in the Student Book.

Section 1: Description

When first reading a text, focus on understanding the events or ideas within it.

Section 2: Information

Section 3: Intention and response

Section 4: Sentence structure for effect

Section 5
Assessment

In this section, you will answer questions on a short extract and improve a sample student response.

▼ **Read the extract and then answer the questions that follow it.**

The Arctic and Antarctic

1 As well as being spectacularly beautiful, the polar regions are amongst the coldest, driest or windiest places on Earth. Bright, white snow and ice stretch as far as the eye can see.

The Arctic

The Arctic is a frozen ocean in the winter surrounded by land. Yet with its vast sea ice, it sprawls over one sixth of the Earth's surface, covering over 30 million km2. The Arctic Ocean is the smallest and shallowest ocean in the world. The
5 ice that forms over it in winter is a giant layer of floating ice. In fact, there is no land at the North Pole, or within many hundreds of kilometres of it.

The Antarctic

At the other end of the Earth, the Antarctic is a frozen land surrounded by ocean. Even in the summer this vast land mass is covered with ice that is an average of 2000 m thick. Antarctica is also a polar desert. At the South Pole, the snowfall is equal to less than 50 mm of rain a year. The Antarctic, much colder than the Arctic, is the coldest place
10 on Earth.

Polar bears

The polar bear of the Arctic is the largest living land carnivore. Polar bears spend over half their time hunting. However, hunting is a difficult task even for the mighty polar bear, which on average will catch only one seal a week. Polar bears depend on the floating sea ice to hunt for seals. However, global warming means that the sea ice is melting earlier and freezing much later in the year. This gives polar bears less time to hunt. Sometimes they have to swim for up to nine
15 days to find sea ice.

Penguins

Penguins are a group of flightless seabirds found in the southern hemisphere. There are 18 different species of penguin. Only the Adélie and emperor penguins live permanently in Antarctica. In parts of the Antarctic, populations of Adélie penguins have dropped by 65 per cent over the past 25 years. Climate change and warming temperatures mean that the atmosphere in Antarctica holds more moisture and this brings snow. This reduces the land area on which Adélie
20 penguins can nest.

Assessment questions

1 Indicate which of the following statements are true and which are false. Circle T or F for each statement.

A The Arctic is the coldest place on Earth. [T / F]

B The Antarctic is a polar desert. [T / F]

C Polar bears only eat around one penguin per month. [T / F]

D The Arctic Ocean is the shallowest on the planet. [T / F]

E Climate change is causing more snow to fall in the Antarctic. [T / F]

2a Look at the first paragraph of the extract. Write down one word or phrase that shows the writer feels positive about the Arctic and Antarctic.

b Write down three words from the introduction that seem negative about the Arctic and Antarctic.

3 The Arctic and Antarctic are at opposite ends of the planet. How has the writer structured the text to reflect the theme of opposites? Support your answer with evidence from the extract.

4 Look at the following question and read the student's response that follows.

Question: Polar bears are threatened by global warming. How does the writer structure ideas to make this point effectively?

Response: Polar bears are very powerful, but global warming is melting the ice in the Arctic. This means that polar bears have less time to hunt and they have to swim a long way to find sea ice.

a What advice would you give to this student to help them improve their response?

b Write your own improved response to the question in the space below. Continue your answer in your notebook if needed.

Section 6
Argument

In this section, you will practise exploring how a writer expresses a point of view to influence the reader's opinions.

Key points

1 Look at the following sentence from the text on page 28 of the Student Book. Rewrite it in your own words.

You empower kids by teaching them how to do something dangerous, but how to do it safely.

2 Write down the key point delivered in each paragraph of the text.

Paragraph 1:

Paragraph 2:

Paragraph 3:

Paragraph 4:

Paragraph 5:

Paragraph 6:

Viewpoint

3 Which of these sentences is the best summary of the writer's point of view? Place a cross (✗) next to your chosen sentence, then write a sentence or two explaining your choice.

A We should encourage children to take risks in a careful way to prepare them for life.

B We should teach children to use knives and light fires.

Set extension activity

4a Imagine you have been asked to write an article with one of the following two titles.

EITHER: 'Parents should give young people more freedom!'
OR: 'Parents should NOT give young people more freedom!'

Make some notes listing every reason you can think of to support your point of view.

b Now identify the five key points you would make in your article.

Point 1:

Point 2:

Point 3:

Point 4:

Point 5:

Emotive language

5 Look again at the text on page 28 of the Student Book. Tick the following quotations from the text that are examples of the writer using emotive language.

A The kids' faces light up. ☐   **B** He has learnt how to handle a knife. ☐

C Kids were taught to be resourceful and practical. ☐   **D** you love and care for your kids ☐

Structural and grammatical choices

6 The writer uses the following triple structure to present his ideas persuasively:

Let's have fun again. Let's get muddy; let's live a bit more freely.

You have been asked to write an article with the opposite point of view, encouraging people to remain in their houses and be safe. Write a line using a triple structure like the one above.

_____

_____

7a Which of the following are examples of direct address?

A Join me and let's make life a little wilder. ☐

B I remember feeling really excited. ☐

C Remember, we all take risks every day. ☐

D Their future is your future. ☐

b Write three points arguing that young people should stay safe at home. Address the reader directly to make your argument more persuasive.

Point 1: _____

_____

Point 2: _____

_____

Point 3: _____

_____

Determiner-noun-verb agreement

8 Delete the incorrect words in the sentences below, making them grammatically correct.

A Yesterday, the boy [ride/rides/rode/riding] his bike to Anna's house.

B Every week the [people/man/girl/friend] met to discuss plans for the festival.

C Last night I saw [the/an/a/some] woman I had never met before.

D Sometimes people [thought/think/thinks/thinking] I cannot speak.

Set extension activity

9a You are going to write an article arguing that young people should stay at home to stay safe. You could use one of these prompts:

- It is not safe to let young people make their own decisions.
- Young people can learn about danger without taking risks.
- Spending time at home teaches young people important skills.

Where appropriate, try to use:

- emotive language
- a triple structure
- direct address.

Write your article here.

_____

_____

_____

_____

_____

_____

_____

_____

_____

_____

_____

_____

_____

_____

_____

_____

_____

_____

_____

_____

_____

_____

_____

b Look back over what you have written and identify any opportunities to include more emotive language.

Section 7
Newspaper report

In this section, you will practise exploring how writers structure news articles and choose vocabulary to engage the reader's attention.

Structure of articles

1 Look again at the text on page 32 of the Student Book. The first event in the story, in chronological order, is when Matthew Bryce was reported missing in paragraph 3. Write a new opening sentence for the article beginning with that piece of information.

_____

_____

2 The article begins when the surfer believes he is about to die. Why do you think the account starts at that point? Explain your answer.

_____

_____

3a Look at the following summary of key points from a news story. Choose the most dramatic moment and write an opening sentence or two for a report on this story.

A A tree fell through the roof of 49-year-old Mr Bradley's house while he was watching TV.

B A pointed branch missed his head by a few centimetres, giving him the fright of his life.

C 'I'm just so lucky to be alive!' said Mr Bradley.

D The neighbours all helped to clear the tree out of the way.

E His wife joked that the loft had needed clearing out for years.

_____

_____

_____

b Complete the report you started writing in **Activity 4a**. Write one further paragraph, using the information provided.

_____

_____

_____

_____

_____

_____

Set extension activity

4 Look at the example of a newspaper article below. Write notes in the margins, describing the key features and structure used in the article, and their effect. An example has been provided.

MISSION IMPOSSIBLE SAVES GIRLS' LIVES

Headline — engages the reader by suggesting danger.

A group of Year 8 girls trapped in a cave in Yorkshire were just hours from death when rescuers found them in the dark.

The group were reported missing three days ago when they failed to return from a tour of the Bluestone caves. "It was the worst phone call you can imagine," says mum of three Linda, recalling the moment the school got in touch to tell her that her daughter was trapped.

"The cave was filling up with water," said cave tour leader Nick. "The tunnel back out of the cave was already flooded and we were running out of time."

A team from the mountain rescue service abseiled down a vertical shaft into another part of the cave system and managed to work their way round to the stranded group before leading them to the shaft.

"Climbing out was the scariest part," says Amy, aged 12. "The shaft was really narrow and steep and I've always been terrified of heights."

"Hopefully the next school trip will be to a museum or something," says Amy.

High Springs Academy says there are no plans for a repeat tour of the caves.

Vocabulary choices

5 Underline the examples of dramatic language in the following sentences.

a The protester was trembling with rage as she approached the police.

b For a moment, the crowd was silent. Then their roars nearly brought the roof down.

c The circus performers delivered a jaw-dropping, nerve-shredding routine.

6a Rewrite the following sentences by changing the vocabulary to make them more dramatic.

 (i) She struck the ball hard into the back of the net.

_____

 (ii) Several trees are blocking the road after last night's storm.

_____

 (iii) The police chased the gang along the motorway at full speed.

_____

b For each rewritten sentence from **Activity 6a**, explain how your vocabulary choices have made it more dramatic.

 (i) _____

 _____

 (ii) _____

 _____

 (iii) _____

 _____

Present tense

7 Rewrite each of these headlines in the present tense.

a Teenager broke world record!

_____

b Dog saved owner from cow

_____

c Woman survived thirty-metre fall

_____

Set extension activity

8a Write a news article about the damage caused to a town by a hurricane. Think about what happened, when and where it happened and who was affected. Remember to include a dramatic headline, the details of what happened and some dramatic vocabulary.

Headline
Main text

b Look back through what you have written and try to find opportunities to choose even more dramatic vocabulary.

Section 8
Comparing texts

In this section, you will practise exploring two magazine articles. You will identify key points in both texts, and compare similarities or differences in the experiences described.

Key points of texts

1a Look again at the two extracts on pages 36 and 37 of the Student Book. Which of the following statements are true of the writer in Extract A? Which are true of the writer in Extract B? Which are true of both? Write 'A', 'B' or 'Both' next to each statement.

A He waits to be rescued after the fall _____

B He acts quickly to save himself _____

C He suffers a painful fall _____

D He is afraid that he is going to die _____

E He is in pain _____

b Indicate which of the following statements are true and which are false. Circle T or F for each statement.

A Both writers lose their phones. [T / F]

B Both writers are injured. [T / F]

C Both writers are in darkness after their falls. [T / F]

D Both writers shout for help. [T / F]

2 What similarities are there in the way that the two writers respond to their situations? Write a short paragraph explaining your answer.

_____

_____

_____

_____

_____

3 What differences can you detect in the attitude each writer had to his situation? Write a short paragraph explaining your answer.

_____

_____

_____

_____

Set extension activity

4a Think of two places that you know well and note these in the space provided. Try to choose places that have quite a few similarities and differences.

My chosen places are: _____

b Identify three to five key differences and three to five key similarities between the two places. Write them in the boxes below. You could write about: the people who go there, the surroundings, and so on.

Key differences
1
2
3
4
5

Key similarities
1
2
3
4
5

Using evidence

5 Look at the following quotations from Extract B on page 37 of the Student Book. Underline the one which best demonstrates that the writer of Extract B feels his situation is hopeless.

A   It felt like being on a waterslide

B   I panicked

C   I started crying

6 Look at the two statements below. Look back at the extracts on pages 36 and 37 of the Student Book and find one or two short quotations that give evidence to support each statement. Write your quotations beneath each statement. Remember to use speech marks around the quotations.

a The writer of Extract A tried to save himself.

_____

_____

_____

b The writer of Extract B waited to be rescued.

_____

_____

_____

7 Now write a paragraph describing this difference between the two writers' attitudes, using the best quotations you have found and linking your points with adverbials.

_____

_____

_____

_____

_____

_____

_____

_____

_____

_____

Using adverbials

8 Add a suitable adverbial to complete the points below.

A The bedroom in my old house was huge. Here in the new house, _____, I feel like I'm living in a shoe box.

B Our camping trip last summer was great! We stayed by a lake and hired canoes. _____, this year we are camping by the water again.

Set extension activity

9 Find two different articles, either online or in magazines or newspapers, on a similar topic. Write a comparison of the two articles.

a Note down three key similarities and differences with suitable quotations from the texts as evidence.

Key similarities	Quotations
1	
2	
3	

Key differences	Quotations
1	
2	
3	

b Write your comparison here, linking your points with adverbials where appropriate. Continue in your notebook if needed.

This section links to pages 40–43 of the Student Book.

Section 9
Letters

In this section, you will practise exploring the conventions of letters. You will then use these to write your own letter about an experience you've had.

Identifying key information

1 Look at the text on page 40 of the Student Book. Indicate which of the following statements are true and which are false. Circle T or F for each statement.

A Penny's brother is not with her because he is ill.   [T / F]

B Penny arranges to meet the girl who lives next door at the beach.   [T / F]

C Penny sees a man who seems to be struggling in the tide.   [T / F]

D Penny is not surprised that she acted so calmly.   [T / F]

Writers' intentions

2 Chronologically, the story ends with Penny appearing on TV. Why do you think she chose to begin her letter by saying that she had been on TV? Explain your answer below.

_____

_____

_____

_____

First and third person

3 Which of these sentences are written in the first person? Which are written in the third person? Write '1st' or '3rd' next to each one.

A I ran for the bus but it was no use.   _____

B She wondered who the strange woman was.   _____

C They laughed at me out of the back window.   _____

4 Rewrite this extract from the letter using the third person, as if you were describing events that happened to a friend or relative.

I've spent the last week visiting my grandma in her cottage by the sea. On the day I arrived, I felt a bit lonely because my brother was too ill to come with me. I didn't think it'd be much fun playing on the beach all by myself!

_____

_____

_____

Set extension activity

5 Make a list of verbs in the table below, writing each verb in the first person and third person, and in the present tense and past tense. Aim to list at least ten to fifteen verbs. An example is provided.

First person present	Third person present	First person past	Third person past
I write	she writes	I wrote	she wrote

Presenting and organising a letter

6 The letter below was intended to be a formal letter of complaint. Look through it carefully and circle any words or features that do not conform to the proper way of presenting a letter, or are missing entirely. In the margin, write notes indicating how you would correct the mistakes.

November   *The date should be complete with day and year*

Hello Sir,

I was very disappointed with the chair that I ordered from your website.

It fell apart as soon as my cousin sat on it. Please give me my money back immediately.

Thanks,
Tom
22 Broke Lane
Oxford
OX4 4OX

7 Rewrite the letter about the broken chair, making the corrections that you have identified.

_____

_____

_____

_____

_____

_____

_____

_____

_____

_____

_____

_____

_____

_____

Set extension activity

8 Write a longer, more detailed version of the letter of complaint from **Activity 7**. Include as much detail as you can about your original order, what happened, exactly how the chair broke, how you feel and what you hope the company will do for you. Remember to:

- use the correct format and layout for a letter
- use a first-person viewpoint
- use a variety of sentence starts in your writing.

Section 10
Reviewing and revising

In this section, you will further develop your skills in reviewing the accuracy and effectiveness of your writing, and revising it to make improvements.

Checking spelling, punctuation and grammar

1 Look at the following sentences and circle the mistakes in each one. Then rewrite each sentence correctly.

a they had never seen an elephant before, they were amazed.

_____

b I could see he was bleeding, I ran over to help

_____

c It was her first ever birthday party. she was so excited

_____

Verb suffixes

2 Circle the verbs in the table below that are spelt incorrectly.

flap	flapped	flapping
stomp	stompped	stompping
reload	reloadded	reloadding
chat	chatted	chatting

Proofreading

3 The following three instructions are mixed up and incorrect. Rewrite them to create useful tips for proofreading your work.

a To find **punctuation mistakes,** look at each verb.

_____

b To find **spelling mistakes,** look at full stops and capital letters.

_____

c To find **grammar mistakes,** look at words with suffixes.

_____

Set extension activity

Having completed the proofreading activities on page 45 of the Student Book, decide which area you most need to focus on: punctuation, spelling or grammar.

4a Write a test for someone else to practise their reviewing skills in that area.

Write instructions for the person sitting the test, telling them what sorts of errors they should look for and correct (punctuation, spelling or grammar).

Then write some text with lots of errors in it. The text could be a list of single sentences that are not linked or it could be a paragraph of text.

Whichever approach you take, the sentences or paragraph must contain at least five mistakes in your chosen area of punctuation, spelling or grammar.

TEST

b Now rewrite the sentences or paragraph with all of the mistakes corrected.

Reviewing vocabulary choice

5 Look at the following sentences. Each has one word underlined and some replacement words suggested in the box beneath the sentence. Rewrite each sentence, improving it by replacing the underlined word with one from the box.

a The storm outside was <u>bad</u>. | violent | loud | ugly | evil |

b The tiger bared its <u>big</u> teeth and growled. | shiny | white | savage | dirty |

c She was <u>tense</u> with anger. | sore | mad | anxious | trembling |

6 Look at this extract from a student's writing. Underline any words or phrases that you think could be replaced to improve the paragraph. Then rewrite the extract including your improvements.

> The chase was on! In front of us the black van was driving through the streets, swerving quickly every now and then to overtake. We went after them, seriously trying to keep up. None of us felt like thinking about if these people got away. My heart was beating. We had to stop them!

Improving your work

7 Write down one useful tip to help you avoid repetition in your writing.

8 What are the four key things to check for when you review your writing?

1 _____

2 _____

3 _____

4 _____

Set extension activity

9 Revise the skills you have covered in the second half of this unit, ready for the assessment in the next lesson. You may find it helpful to note down the key points covered in each of the sections so far. If there are any areas where you do not feel confident, reread the information given in the Student Book throughout this unit. Think back to when you planned for the previous assessment. What helped? What could you improve on?

Section 6: Argument

Each paragraph in an argument text will contain one key point.

_____

_____

_____

_____

Section 7: Newspaper report

_____

_____

_____

_____

_____

Section 8: Comparing texts

_____

_____

_____

_____

Section 9: Letters

_____

_____

_____

_____

_____

Section 10: Reviewing and revising

_____

_____

_____

_____

Section 11
Assessment

In this section, you will identify the mistakes in a sample response from a student and write an improved version.

1 Look at the following task and read the student's response that follows.

Task:: Imagine a story about a character who faces a situation in which they may die. Write an extract from this scene.

Response: We have been walking for three hours by the time the sun came up. We were happy because we had been walking for three hours and we liked the feel of the weight coming off our feet because now that our boots could no longer be heard the carm of the mountain was nice. Everything feels carm and nice and at peace

Then we heard a huge sound like a blender and high above us just below the peak, a huge bit of the white separated from the mountain and seemed to fall and we were all really tired.

"Avalanche!" someone said and we got back to our feet. It was obvious we wouldn't' make it. We stomped like elephants in mud. The avalanche got even more quicker. It was swept up more and more snow as it raced down the mountainside. then I triped and now I too was racing down the mountain on my chest.

You are going to improve and extend this response.

a Underline any spelling or punctuation mistakes.
b Underline any verbs that are in the wrong tense.
c Write a 'V' next to any opportunities to improve the impact of the writing by making different vocabulary choices.
d Write an 'S' next to any opportunities to improve the impact of the writing by varying sentence length and structure.
e Use the space in the box below to make some notes and plan how you will improve and extend this answer.

2 Write your improved version of the answer in the space below. Remember to:

- be clear about the effect on the reader you want to create
- choose powerful, dramatic vocabulary
- use a variety of sentence structures for effect.

Section 1
Reading and understanding

In this section, you will practise exploring different ways of reading a text and identify key points of information.

Skimming a text

1 Read the extract on page 52 of the Student Book, which is broken up into four sections. For each section, write one sentence summarising the topic of that section of the extract.

a Section 1 _____

_____

b Section 2 _____

_____

c Section 3 _____

_____

d Section 4 _____

_____

2 Circle T or F to indicate which of the statements below are true or false. Then, in the space beneath each statement, write one sentence explaining your answer.

A The text is written to entertain the reader. [T / F]

_____

_____

B The text is written to inform the reader. [T / F]

_____

_____

C The text is written to warn the reader. [T / F]

_____

_____

D The text is written to express the writer's opinion. [T / F]

_____

_____

Set extension activity

3a Research tsunamis, either online or in other sources, using the skimming skills you have learnt. Write down as many interesting facts as you can find.

_____

_____

_____

_____

_____

_____

_____

_____

_____

_____

_____

_____

_____

_____

_____

_____

_____

_____

_____

_____

_____

_____

_____

_____

b Think of at least three subheadings you could use to group your facts under that would help readers to skim-read your text and get an overview of the content. Write your subheadings in the space below.

_____

_____

_____

_____

Scanning a text

4 Read questions A–E below and for each one:
a Write down one or two key words from the question that you can use to scan the extract on page 52 of the Student Book.
b Write a sentence answering the question once you have scanned the extract for your key words.

A What should you make in preparation for a tsunami?

Key words: _____

Answer: _____

_____

B Where should you move during a tsunami?

Key words: _____

Answer: _____

_____

C Why should you never go to the water to watch a tsunami?

Key words: _____

Answer: _____

_____

D Why should you not return home until told to do so after a tsunami?

Key words: _____

Answer: _____

_____

E What should you stay away from after a tsunami?

Key words: _____

Answer: _____

Combining key points

5 Scan the extract on page 52 of the Student Book and note down any information about where you should and should not go before, during and after a tsunami.

_____

_____

_____

_____

_____

Set extension activity

6 You are going to write a guide explaining how and why you should skim and scan texts. Refer back to pages 53–55 of the Student Book to remind yourself of the range of techniques.

a Make notes as you read through the Student Book pages, writing down any information or tips that could be included in your guide.

_____

_____

_____

_____

_____

_____

_____

_____

_____

_____

b Now write your guide, using appropriate subheadings to make it easier for readers to skim and scan your text.

_____

_____

_____

_____

_____

_____

_____

_____

_____

_____

_____

_____

_____

_____

_____

_____

_____

_____

Section 2
Combining key points

In this section, you will practise exploring key ideas the writer has used to create a tense description.

Decoding unfamiliar words

1 Read the following sentences and look at the underlined words. For each underlined word, decide which of the suggested definitions makes the most sense. Circle the definition you select.

a During the school council election, the <u>calibre</u> of the speeches was very high.

- quality
- volume
- tone
- excitement

b I remember my first sight of the tsunami very clearly. At first the wave looked a little bigger than average. There was no sign of the <u>catastrophe</u> we were about to experience.

- excitement
- surprise
- disaster
- pain

c It was the wave's <u>velocity</u> that most took me by surprise. One moment it seemed to be on the horizon. The next it was crashing through the village.

- height
- depth
- speed
- colour

d The house withstood the first battering by the wave. Then, as the water swirled around it, the building seemed to <u>implode</u>.

- fall in on itself
- disappear
- grow
- shrink

e My neighbour was in shock. She ran out of her house, <u>gesticulating</u> wildly.

- howling
- singing loudly
- chatting fast
- using gestures dramatically

Set extension activity

2 Look back through Units 1 and 2 of the Student Book. Note down any unusual words in the space below. These could be words that you did not understand the first time you read them, or words that you think some other students might not understand. Look up each word in a dictionary and write down the definition in the space below. Then write a sentence of your own, using the word.

Word	
Definition	
Sentence	
Word	
Definition	
Sentence	
Word	
Definition	
Sentence	
Word	
Definition	
Sentence	
Word	
Definition	
Sentence	
Word	
Definition	
Sentence	
Word	
Definition	
Sentence	
Word	
Definition	
Sentence	
Word	
Definition	
Sentence	

Combining key points

3 Note down four key points about Ning Nong the elephant and the people from the extract on page 56 of the Student Book. Use the questions below as prompts.

a How does Ning Nong show that he knows the tsunami is coming?

_____

_____

b How do the humans show that they do not know the tsunami is coming?

_____

_____

c How does Ning Nong save Amber's life?

_____

_____

d How do Amber and her mother and stepfather escape the tsunami?

_____

_____

4 Now write two paragraphs comparing Ning Nong's instincts to the humans' instincts. Remember to use comparative language to link the points that you make. For example: _like, unlike, however, similarly, on the other hand_.

_____

_____

_____

_____

_____

_____

_____

_____

_____

_____

_____

_____

_____

Set extension activity

5 You are going to write two paragraphs describing your feelings about a competition you have taken part in, for example, a sports event or a TV talent show. The competition could be real or imaginary.

a Note down three to five things you found exciting about taking part in the competition.

b Write a paragraph combining the points you have noted down.

c Note down three to five things that made you feel nervous or tense during the competition.

d Write a paragraph combining the points you have noted down to summarise the feelings you experienced.

e Look back over what you have written. Where possible, improve your writing by adding in comparative vocabulary to link your points.

Section 3
Summarising key information

In this section, you will practise identifying key ideas and using them to write a summary.

Identifying and summarising key points

1 Look again at the extract in Section 2 on page 56 of the Student Book. You are going to create a summary of the text describing Amber and Ning Nong surviving the tsunami.

a Note down all the key points, ideas or events in the space below.

_____

_____

_____

_____

_____

_____

_____

_____

b Now write your own summary of what happened to Amber, based on the points you noted down in the previous activity. Your summary should not be longer than the allocated space.

_____

_____

_____

_____

_____

_____

_____

c Look back through what you have written for **Activity 1b** and identify the essential points, without which the story does not make sense. Now write the shortest possible summary, including only the essential points.

_____

_____

_____

Set extension activity

2a Imagine that you have found out that a large river close to your home is in danger of overflowing, causing a flood. Use the space below to note down everything you can think of that could be dangerous about a flood.

_____

_____

_____

_____

_____

_____

_____

_____

_____

_____

_____

_____

_____

_____

_____

_____

_____

_____

_____

b Now select the key points from **Activity 2a** and combine them to write a summary of the dangers of a flood, using a maximum of five sentences.

_____

_____

_____

_____

_____

_____

_____

_____

_____

Writing a summary

3 Look at the following bullet points, some of which you could use to summarise the story of Red Riding Hood.

- Red Riding Hood is having breakfast at home.
- She decides to go and visit her sick grandmother.
- Her grandmother lives on the other side of the forest.
- Her mother tells her to stick to the path in the forest.
- Red Riding Hood packs a basket of food and sets off to visit her grandmother.
- It is a fine day and she is in a good mood.
- In the forest, she gets the feeling that someone is following her.
- In the forest, a wolf asks her where she is going and she tells him.
- The wolf suggests that she pick some flowers to cheer her grandmother up.
- Red Riding Hood finds lots of pretty flowers.
- The wolf runs ahead to the grandmother's house, eats her and lies in wait, disguised as the grandmother.
- Red Riding Hood does not suspect that anything is wrong.
- Red Riding Hood arrives and the wolf eats her before falling asleep.
- A woodcutter rescues Red Riding Hood and her grandmother by cutting the wolf open.
- Red Riding Hood is very relieved!

Copy out the points that are essential facts from the list above, without which the story does not make sense.

_____

_____

_____

_____

_____

_____

_____

_____

_____

_____

_____

4 Based on the key points you have identified, write a short summary of the story, using no more than 50 words.

_____

_____

_____

_____

_____

Set extension activity

5a Write down all the key points from a well-known story of your choice.

_____
_____
_____
_____
_____
_____
_____
_____
_____
_____
_____
_____
_____
_____
_____
_____
_____
_____
_____
_____

b Condense these points into a maximum of five essential points, without which the story would not make sense.

_____
_____
_____
_____
_____

c Write a short summary of the story, using no more than 50 words.

_____
_____
_____
_____

Section 4
Comparing key points

In this section, you will practise identifying and comparing the key ideas in two texts.

Identifying key points

1 Use the following questions as prompts to help you note down some of the key points from Extract A on page 64 of the Student Book.

a How do Anna and her mother know that they are in danger?

_____

_____

b What happens when the water sweeps across the road?

_____

_____

c How do Anna and her mother feel at this point?

_____

_____

d How do the mother's emotions change as they drive away from the water?

_____

_____

e How do Anna and her mother feel when they are in the hotel room?

_____

_____

2 Write a paragraph answering the following question: How does Anna react to the disaster?

_____

_____

_____

_____

_____

_____

_____

Set extension activity

3a Note down the key facts and events described in Extract A on page 64 of the Student Book, in chronological order, including how Anna and her mother feel and react as the disaster unfolds.

_____

_____

_____

_____

_____

_____

_____

_____

_____

_____

_____

_____

_____

_____

_____

_____

_____

_____

_____

_____

_____

_____

_____

b Now write a paragraph comparing the reactions of Anna to those of her mother.

_____

_____

_____

_____

_____

_____

_____

_____

_____

_____

Comparing key points

4 Look again at the extract about Amber and Ning Nong the elephant in Section 2 on page 56 of the Student Book.

Make notes summarising the key points about how Amber and her mother react to the tsunami. Include both emotional and physical responses.

_____

_____

_____

_____

_____

_____

5 You are going to compare the two extracts you have looked at in **Activities 1–4** on pages 58–60 of this Workbook and the way that the characters react to the natural disasters in those extracts.

a In the table below, note down the key differences and similarities between the extracts.

Key similarities	Key differences

b Now write a paragraph comparing the way in which the characters react to the natural disasters in the two extracts.

_____

_____

_____

_____

_____

_____

_____

Set extension activity

6 Revise the skills you have covered in the first half of this unit, ready for the assessment in the next lesson. You may find it helpful to note down the key points covered in each of the sections so far. If there are any areas where you do not feel confident, reread the appropriate pages in the Student Book.

Section 1: Reading and understanding

To skim-read a text, look at the headings and the first sentence in each paragraph.

Section 2: Combining key points

Section 3: Summarising key information

Section 4: Comparing key points

Section 5
Assessment

In this section, you will answer questions on a short extract and improve a sample student response.

▼ Read the extract and then answer the questions that follow it.

1 It was late evening and the sounds of the forest had changed. The wind had dropped and the air was still. Birdsong trilled around the canopy, but underneath those sounds was a silence that Sam enjoyed. It was as if, at the point between day and night, the forest had paused to rest.

Sam could not afford to pause – the cabin was still two miles away and he did not want to be on the trail after dark. He
5 wiped the sweat from his eyes and pressed forward at a light jog. The act of running sent a tingle up Sam's spine as imaginary bears began to chase him along the trail. He ran faster. Ahead he saw a small clearing.

And on the other side of the clearing, he saw the wolf.

It sat facing him in the middle of the trail. Sam skidded to a standstill, a lump rising in his throat. What had the leaflet said? Something about trying to make yourself look bigger. Sam stood tall and held his arms outstretched.

10 The wolf's hindquarters rose slowly, tautly, as if pushing up against a weight. The head lowered slightly.

What now? 'Walk slowly backwards away from the wolf', the leaflet had said. He couldn't go back and wait. He had to get to the cabin before dark. He couldn't bear the idea of facing the silent dangers of the forest in the dark. Swallowing hard, Sam took a step forward. The wolf's eyes never left his. He took another step. The wolf growled and the hair around its neck bristled.

15 Sam felt his own neck prickling in response. 'As a last resort, shout and throw things at the wolf'. He reached down and his trembling fingers closed around a stick.

"AWAY!" he shrieked as he hurled the stick at the wolf. The stick spun through the air. The wolf's eyes remained locked on his. With a snarl, it sprang at him.

Assessment questions

1 What three pieces of advice from a leaflet does Sam recall?

_____

_____

_____

2 Which three of the following are key points of information in the extract? Circle the correct answers.

A Sam is hurrying towards the cabin. **B** Sam is afraid of bears.
C Sam encounters a wolf. **D** The wolf attacks.

3 Write a summary of the extract in no more than 50 words.

_____

_____

_____

_____

4 Find and write down three quotations from the extract that show how Sam feels. For each one, explain what the quotation suggests about Sam's emotions.

_____

_____

_____

_____

5 Look at the following question and read the student's response that follows.

Question: How do Sam's thoughts and feelings change throughout the extract on page 62?

Response: Sam is really scared because he is alone in the woods and it is getting dark and there might be bears. Then he meets a wolf and tries to scare it away because he remembers reading some advice in a leaflet but it isn't scared and it attacks him.

a What advice would you give to this student to help them improve their response?

_____

_____

_____

_____

b Write your own improved response to the question in the space below.

_____

_____

_____

_____

_____

_____

_____

_____

Section 6
Inferring intentions

In this section, you will practise your inference skills and use them to explore a writer's intention.

Retrieving key information

1 Find the correct information from the extract on page 70 of the Student Book to answer these questions.

a What three things are listed that could cause a fire near the house?

_____

_____

_____

b What reason did Mum give for joining the volunteer fire crew?

_____

c List two changes that Brin has noticed in his mother's appearance.

_____

_____

Using inference

2a Look at paragraph 4 of the extract on page 70 of the Student Book. What does the following sentence suggest about Brin's emotions? Brin paced around the house, unable to relax.

_____

_____

b Look at paragraph 5 of the extract and select three phrases that suggest how Brin feels. For each phrase, write a sentence including the quotation and an explanation of what it suggests about Brin's emotions.

_____

_____

_____

_____

_____

Set extension activity

3 Complete the boxes below by:

- writing your own definitions of the terms 'imply', 'infer' and 'explicit'
- finding and explaining one example from your study of the extract on page 70 of the Student Book (for example: 'He ran to the door and threw it open.' This implies that he is anxious and eager for news about his mum.)
- making up an example of your own.

Imply
Definition: _____ _____
Example from the text: _____ _____
Your own example: _____ _____

Infer
Definition: _____ _____
Example from the text: _____ _____
Your own example: _____ _____

Explicit
Definition: _____ _____
Example from the text: _____ _____
Your own example: _____ _____

Inferring the writer's intention

4a Write down every phrase you can find from the extract on page 70 of the Student Book that demonstrates the writer intends to show the reader that Brin is worried about his mother.

_____

_____

_____

_____

_____

_____

_____

_____

_____

b Now choose two or three phrases from **Activity 4a**. Write one or two sentences to explain how you know that the writer intends to show the reader that Brin is worried. Include the phrases you chose as evidence.

_____

_____

_____

_____

How to imply meaning in your writing

5 Look at the sentences below. Rewrite each one so that the meaning is implied rather than stated. An example is provided:

She was annoyed because I was late.
She was checking her watch, tapping her foot and frowning.

a The dog was so happy to see me.

_____

b He was annoyed with himself for forgetting his phone.

_____

c She was terrified.

_____

d Everyone in the room was nervous.

_____

Set extension activity

6 You are going to write two or three paragraphs of a story in which you show that the narrator is waiting at a bus station and becoming more and more anxious.

a First, make some notes using the following questions as prompts.

(i) What could the narrator be nervous about?

_____

_____

_____

(ii) What words would you use to state the narrator's feelings? For example: *anxious, nervous, afraid.*

_____

_____

(iii) Write down how you could show these emotions without stating them? For example: *nervous: fiddled with her necklace.*

_____

_____

_____

_____

b Now write your description, remembering to imply the narrator's emotions rather than state them. Continue your answer in your notebook if needed.

_____

_____

_____

_____

_____

_____

_____

_____

_____

_____

_____

_____

_____

Section 7
Responding to a text

In this section, you will practise exploring your response to a text and identifying the writer's intention.

Exploring your first response to a text

1 Read the extract on page 74 of the Student Book and answer these questions.

a Why do you think Sunflower wanted to go to Damaidi? Write one or two sentences, using quotations from the extract to support your answer.

_____

_____

_____

_____

_____

b At what point did you start to think that something might go wrong for Sunflower? Write one or two sentences, using quotations from the extract to support your answer.

_____

_____

_____

_____

_____

Identifying the writer's intention

2a Reread the first paragraph. What do you think the writer wants us to think or feel in this paragraph? Answer using one sentence only.

_____

_____

b How does the writer achieve their intention? Write one or two sentences, using quotations to support your answer.

_____

_____

_____

_____

Set extension activity

3 Look again at the 'Intention Bank' on page 75 of the Student Book.

a You are going to create your own version of this list. Note down every possible intention that a writer could have. Think about books you have read, stories you have heard and films or TV programmes you have watched.

b Pick one of the intentions you have noted down and write a paragraph of your own to achieve that intention.

Synonyms and antonyms

4 Complete the table below, adding at least two synonyms and at least one antonym for every word in the left-hand column. An example is provided.

Word	Synonyms	Antonyms
calm	peaceful, tranquil	chaotic, noisy
angry		
interesting		
anxious		
big		
dangerous		
exciting		
pain		
fear		

Writing a response

5 Reread the following paragraph from the extract on page 74 of the Student Book.

> A sailing boat came along. Seeing a little girl clinging to the embankment like a gecko, the man at the helm called out to her. Then, afraid that he might startle her, he stopped – although he worried about her long after he had passed by.

a In one sentence, summarise what is happening in this paragraph.

_____

_____

b Note down any particular words or images from the paragraph that have a powerful effect on the reader.

_____

_____

_____

c Use your answers to **Activities 5a** and **5b** above to write two or three sentences explaining the writer's intention in this paragraph.

_____

_____

_____

_____

_____

_____

Set extension activity

6 Remind yourself of the work you have done in this section of the Workbook and Student Book. Now write a guide for other students explaining how to write a response to a text. Think about how to set out your guide. You may want to use subheadings or examples. Remember to cover:

- the character's thoughts and feelings
- the reader's thoughts and feelings
- the writer's intention
- the writer's use of vocabulary
- use of quotations.

This section links to pages 78–81 of the Student Book.

Section 8
Supporting your response

In this section, you will practise exploring a character's viewpoint and support your response with evidence.

Finding evidence about characters

1a Read the extract on page 78 of the Student Book. Find and write down two sentences from the extract that support the following statement: Lucas was very happy to be in Paris.

_____

_____

_____

b Now select the most powerful phrase from the sentences you have selected and write it below.

_____

c Now write a sentence making the point that Lucas was happy, using your selected phrase as evidence.

_____

_____

2a How did Lucas feel when he realised he had taken a wrong turn? Write down two or three words that summarise Lucas' emotions.

_____

b Write down two sentences from the extract that show Lucas felt this way.

_____

_____

_____

c Now select the most powerful phrase from the sentences and write it below.

_____

d Now write a sentence or two, including the phrase you have selected as evidence, to answer the question: How did Lucas feel when he realised he was lost?

_____

_____

_____

Set extension activity

3 Choose your three favourite stories, either from books or films. For each one, write a paragraph explaining why you enjoyed it. Use examples from the books or films to support the points you make. (You need not search for precise quotations.) For example, you might write: *I really like the character Amy. She is very loyal, which is shown when she goes back to rescue Ravi from the cave.*

Title 1: _____

_____

_____

_____

_____

_____

_____

_____

_____

_____

Title 2: _____

_____

_____

_____

_____

_____

_____

_____

_____

_____

Title 3: _____

_____

_____

_____

_____

_____

_____

_____

_____

Single- and multi-clause sentences

4 How many clauses are there in each of the following sentences? Write the number of clauses next to each sentence.

a I went to the lake and skimmed stones.   _____

b I skimmed stones.   _____

c I skimmed stones across the water.   _____

d The surface of the water was flat and the stones bounced really well.   _____

e It was late so I went home.   _____

5 In each example below, rewrite the sets of single-clause sentences as one multi-clause sentence. Add conjunctions if necessary.

a I saw the shark's fin. It disappeared.

_____

b I was scared now. It was dark. I was lost.

_____

Planning your response to a text

6 You are going to plan and write a response to a fiction text of your choosing. Find a fiction text and read the opening few paragraphs. Make some notes explaining:

a The setting: _____

_____

_____

_____

b What is happening: _____

_____

_____

_____

c What you know about the main character: _____

_____

_____

_____

Set extension activity

7 Continue to plan your response to the opening few paragraphs of a fiction text that you started in **Activity 6** on the previous page.

a What is the overall effect of the text? Write down a few words that sum up the feeling created. For example: *fear, tension, humour, sympathy*.

_____

b Note down any phrases or sentences in the text that link to the words you have noted in **Activity 7a** above.

_____

_____

_____

_____

_____

_____

c Now write your response to the text. Remember to:

- focus on the effect the writer has had on you as the reader
- use short quotations to support the points you make.

_____

_____

_____

_____

_____

_____

_____

_____

_____

_____

_____

_____

_____

_____

_____

Section 9
Developing your response

In this section, you will practise tracking and developing your response to a text.

Tracking your response

1 Look again at the extract in Section 8 on page 78 of the Student Book. Make some notes on each paragraph or section of the extract, answering the following questions:

- What information have you found out from this paragraph or section?
- What are you thinking or feeling after reading this paragraph or section?
- What has made you think and feel that way?

Paragraph 1: _____

_____

_____

_____

Paragraph 2: _____

_____

_____

_____

Paragraph 3: _____

_____

_____

_____

Paragraph 4: _____

_____

_____

_____

The remainder of the extract: _____

_____

_____

_____

Set extension activity

2 Find another fiction text and look at the opening few paragraphs.

Make some notes using the prompts below.

a Who is the main character and what sort of person are they? For example: *young, adventurous, shy, friendly,* etc.

_____

_____

_____

_____

_____

_____

b Where is the story set? What sort of place is it?

_____

_____

_____

_____

_____

_____

c How has the writer made you feel after the first few lines?

_____

_____

_____

_____

_____

d How does the writer continue to make you feel that way as the opening progresses? Or how does the writer create different feelings as the opening progresses?

_____

_____

_____

_____

_____

Writing your response

3 Reread the whole extract on page 78 of the Student Book. Answer the following questions, considering your vocabulary choices carefully.

a Write one or two sentences summing up your response to paragraphs 1 and 2.

_____

_____

b Choose one or two quotations from the extract that show how the writer helped create that response.

_____

_____

c Using quotations to support your point, write one or two sentences explaining how the writer helped create that response, aiming to comment on the writer's choice of vocabulary.

_____

_____

d Write one or two sentences summing up your response to paragraphs 3 and 4.

_____

_____

e Choose one or two quotations from the extract that show how the writer helped create that response.

_____

_____

f Using quotations to support your point, write one or two sentences explaining how the writer helped create that response, aiming to comment on the writer's choice of vocabulary.

_____

_____

g Write one or two sentences summing up your response to the rest of the extract.

_____

_____

h Choose one or two quotations from the extract that show how the writer helped create that response.

_____

_____

i Using quotations to support your point, write one or two sentences explaining how the writer helped create that response, aiming to comment on the writer's choice of vocabulary.

_____

_____

Set extension activity

4 Write three paragraphs in response to the following question: How does your response to the extract change as the extract progresses?

Look back at your answers to **Activity 3** on the previous page and build on these. Remember to:

- comment on how the writer achieves the effects
- focus on the writer's vocabulary choices
- use short quotations from the extract.

Paragraph 1: _____

_____

_____

_____

_____

_____

_____

_____

_____

_____

Paragraph 2: _____

_____

_____

_____

_____

_____

_____

_____

_____

_____

Paragraph 3: _____

_____

_____

_____

_____

_____

_____

_____

Section 10
Writing your response

In this section, you will practise writing the opening of a story and a response to it.

Writing a story opening

1 You are going to plan the opening of your own story set inside a large building. At the beginning you need to create a sense of excitement. This excitement should then turn to a sense of fear by the end of your story opening.

a In the table below, note down any powerful vocabulary that could help you create feelings of excitement and fear.

Excitement	Fear

b Make some notes on what your narrator may think and feel in your story opening. For each thought or feeling, note down how you will imply what they are thinking or feeling. For example: *A picture makes her feel happy and safe: 'She smiled as she remembered looking at the very same picture last year with her mum.'*

Set extension activity

2a Write the opening to your story in the space below. Remember to:

- use powerful vocabulary to create the intended atmosphere
- make sure that the atmosphere changes from excitement to fear
- imply emotions rather than stating them explicitly.

_____

_____

_____

_____

_____

_____

_____

_____

_____

_____

_____

_____

_____

_____

_____

_____

_____

_____

_____

_____

_____

_____

_____

_____

_____

_____

_____

b Look back over what you have written and correct any spelling, punctuation and grammar mistakes. In particular, check that:

- verbs ending in -s, -ed and -ing are correct
- every sentence begins with a capital latter and ends with a full stop, a question mark or an exclamation mark
- you have not joined any full sentences with a comma
- every verb agrees with its subject
- every verb matches the tense used in the rest of the writing.

Writing your response

3a You are now going to write a response to the story opening you wrote for **Activity 2a** on the previous page. Aim to write two paragraphs. The first should explore the atmosphere of excitement. The second should explore the atmosphere of fear.

In each paragraph:
- state how the story made you feel
- select one or two short quotations that made you feel that way
- explain how they had this effect.

b Now that you have completed your response, how might you improve the story opening you wrote to better achieve the effects of excitement and fear? Note down your thoughts in the space below.

Set extension activity

4 Revise the skills you have covered in the second half of this unit, ready for the assessment in the next lesson. You may find it helpful to note down the key points covered in each of the sections so far. If there are any areas where you do not feel confident, reread the appropriate pages in the Student Book. Think back to when you planned for the previous assessment. What helped? What could you improve on?

Section 6: Inferring intentions

To retrieve the key information from a text, use your skim-reading and scanning skills.

_____

_____

_____

_____

Section 7: Responding to a text

_____

_____

_____

_____

_____

Section 8: Supporting your response

_____

_____

_____

_____

_____

Section 9: Developing your response

_____

_____

_____

_____

_____

Section 10: Writing your response

_____

_____

_____

_____

Section 11
Assessment

In this section, you will identify the mistakes in a sample student response and write an improved version.

▼ Read the extract and then answer the questions that follow it.

1 The nearer I got to that house, the drearier it appeared. It seemed like the one wing of a house that had never been finished. What should have been the inner end stood open on the upper floors, and showed against the sky with steps and stairs of uncompleted **masonry**[1]. Many of the windows were unglazed, and bats flew in and out like doves out of a dove-cote.

5 The night had begun to fall as I got close; and in three of the lower windows, which were very high up and narrow, and well barred, the changing light of a little fire began to glimmer. Was this the palace I had been coming to? Was it within these walls that I was to seek new friends and begin great fortunes? Why, in my father's house on Essen-Waterside, the fire and the bright lights would show a mile away, and the door open to a beggar's knock!

   I came forward cautiously, and giving ear as I came, heard someone rattling with dishes, and a little dry, eager cough
10 that came in fits; but there was no sound of speech, and not a dog barked.

Key vocabulary

masonry[1]: bricks or stone for building

1 Look at the following question and sample student response.

> **Question:** What effect is the writer trying to create in these paragraphs?

> **Response:** The narator didnt like the way the house looks because there are bats everywere and its a bit spooky and he wishes he was at home at his fathers house. But theirs a fire because its a palace and he knows he would find friends inside. He hear someone coughing inside but we don't no weather they can speak and theirs no dog.
>
> I like how the hole thing feels really dark and scary.

You are going to improve and extend this response.

a Underline any spelling or punctuation mistakes.
b Underline any verbs that are in the wrong tense.
c Write a 'V' next to any opportunities to improve the impact of the writing by making different vocabulary choices.
d Write an 'S' next to any opportunities to improve the impact of the writing by varying sentence length and structure.
e Use the space in the box on page 85 to make some notes and plan how you will improve and extend this answer.

2 Write your improved version of the answer in the space below. Continue your answer in your notebook if needed. Remember to:

- use quotations
- describe your own response
- comment on how the writer created that effect
- write at least three paragraphs.

Section 1
Creating an impression

In this section, you will practise exploring the ideas and information suggested by a text and the impression the writer has tried to create.

Understanding events

1 Look again at the extract on page 94 of the Student Book and answer the following questions.

a What wakes Hiroyuki?

_____

b How does the girl open Hiroyuki's sleep pod?

_____

c What has happened to the other people on the ship?

_____

d Who is Passenger 72350?

_____

e What does Pilot X7 tell Hiroyuki to do?

_____

Making inferences

2a Look at the sentences below, which are taken from the extract. Write one word underneath each sentence to summarise what you infer about Hiroyuki's feelings. You could choose from the suggestions below or use your own ideas.

happy | sad | uncomfortable | worried | comfortable | excited | nervous | confused | bored | alarmed

(i) Hiroyuki peered timidly through the open door into the silent shadows of a dark corridor.

_____

(ii) "What do you want?" mumbled Hiroyuki. "Are we nearly there yet? Is something wrong?"

_____

(iii) Hiroyuki's eyes narrowed. "But my mum," he said, turning to her sleep pod beside his.

_____

b Look back at the extract and identify the order in which Hiroyuki's feelings are suggested. Write 1, 2 or 3 next to the feelings you wrote above to reflect the order you have identified.

Set extension activity

3a Write a description of a character, creating the impression that they are increasingly anxious. Remember, you can show that they are anxious by describing what they say or how they act, rather than by stating explicitly how they feel. For example: *Ryan sucked in a lungful of air and blew it out again slowly, trying to slow his racing heart.*

b Now write a description of a second character in a similar situation, creating the impression that they are very confident and arrogant. Again, do not state explicitly how the character thinks or feels.

c Choose one of your descriptions and answer the following question: How have you created the impression that this character is anxious or arrogant?

Connotations

4a Look at the following sentence from the extract on page 94 of the Student Book and underline the three words that have connotations of tension and anxiety.

> "Come on," she hissed urgently through clenched teeth.

b Rewrite the sentence above, replacing the word 'hissed' with a different verb to make the girl sound angry rather than anxious.

_____

c Rewrite the sentence again, replacing the adverb 'urgently' to make the girl seem dangerous rather than anxious.

_____

d Looking again at the original sentence, answer the following question: How have the vocabulary choices made by the writer created an impression of the girl's character?

_____

_____

_____

Creating impressions

5 You are going to plan the opening to your own short story about the same characters you have read about on page 94 of the Student Book. The spaceship has just landed on a distant planet and Hiroyuki and the girl are stepping outside. Think about the impression you want to create of the characters, for example, *cautious*, *frightened*, *bold*, *confident*. Then think about the kind of actions and dialogue that would create your intended impressions. Note down your ideas in the table below. Continue your answer in your notebook if needed.

	Hiroyuki	The girl
Characteristics		
Action		
Dialogue		

Set extension activity

6a Continue to plan the opening to the story you started in **Activity 5**. Think about what impression you want to create of the planet. Does it seem like a hostile or welcoming environment? Make notes below listing some details about the setting. Try to use some adjectives that help to create your intended impression. For example: a *warm* glow; *dark, looming* mountains.

b Now write the opening two or three paragraphs of your story, using the planning notes you made for **Activities 5 and 6a**. Remember to focus on creating clear impressions of the setting and the characters using dialogue, action and description.

c Look back over what you have written and make any improvements you can by using vocabulary that has stronger connotations of the feeling or characteristic you want to suggest.

Section 2
Exploring intention and structure

In this section, you will practise exploring the structure of a description from a fiction text, and the effect that the writer wanted it to have on the reader.

Making inferences

1 Look at the following sentences taken from the extract on page 98 of the Student Book.

> Stopping just before the doorway, he realised that his heart was skipping but the sound of his own pulse was loud and slow in his ears.

> He walked in, doing his best to seem confident.

a Underline the words or sentence that suggests what Cas thinks of himself.

b Using at least one quotation from the sentences above, explain what you can infer about the way Cas sees or thinks about himself.

_____

_____

> Cas realised that they might be the first people to have ever had this view. All at once he felt tiny, an insignificant speck in front of this vast awe-inspiring sight.

c Underline the words or sentence that suggests how Cas feels at this moment.

d Using at least one quotation from the sentences above, explain what you can infer about the way Cas feels at this moment.

_____

_____

Intention and response

2 Openings to novels often suggest unanswered questions in the reader's mind so that they want to read on to find out more. Read these sentences from the extract and answer the questions that follow.

> A dream sat on the edge of his thoughts – a white horse surrounded by maple trees – but he couldn't keep hold of it. Something to do with home?

a What question do you think the writer wants you to ask at this point?

_____

b Thinking about the whole extract on page 98 of the Student Book, what other unanswered questions does the writer intend to create in the reader's mind?

_____

_____

Set extension activity

3 You are going to write the opening paragraph or two for your own story about a dream containing one main character, with the intention of making readers wonder whether or not the dream was real. Try to create unanswered questions like those you identified in the extract on page 98 of the Student Book. Make notes on the following:

a What the dream is about

_____

_____

_____

b How the character feels

_____

_____

_____

c Clues that it might or might not be a dream

_____

_____

_____

d Unanswered questions you want to create

_____

_____

_____

4 Now write your opening in the space below.

_____

_____

_____

_____

_____

_____

_____

_____

_____

_____

_____

_____

Paragraphing

5 Look at paragraphs 3 and 4 of the extract on page 98 of the Student Book. Why has the writer started a new paragraph at 'They turned to him'?

Structure

6a Look at the second half of the extract on page 98 of the Student Book beginning '...and suddenly he felt cold.' There are five paragraphs in this section including the sentence above. In which paragraphs does the writer state or suggest the characters' thoughts and feelings?

b Why do you think the writer has chosen to structure the paragraphs in this way?

c Imagine that the writer had structured the paragraphs differently, with one section on thoughts and feelings and another section on action and description. Would this have improved the passage of text? It may help to consider your answer to **Activity 6b** above. Explain your answer below.

Planning

7 You are going to plan a piece of writing describing the pilot of a spacecraft approaching an unknown planet where he must land to find fuel. Make some notes using the prompts below.

a What can the pilot see inside and outside the spacecraft?

b What are the pilot's thoughts and feelings?

Set extension activity

8a You are going to finish planning and then write the description you began planning in **Activity 7**. Make notes on how you will structure the piece. Ensure that you include these elements:

- descriptions of the setting
- references to the senses
- descriptions of thoughts and feelings throughout.

b Now write the piece you have planned.

Section 3
Selecting verbs

In this section, you will practise exploring the importance of selecting precise and powerful verbs in descriptive writing.

Inference

1a Look at the final paragraph of the article on page 102 of the Student Book. Write down the phrase that suggests it is very difficult to complete the training.

b Look through the rest of the article and write down three other phrases or sentences that suggest the training is extremely difficult.

Looking at verb choice

2 Look at the following section from the article on page 102 of the Student Book.

'…it's time to release yourself from the harness, escape through the cabin window, and swim to the surface.'

The writer could have chosen to write 'get out' instead of 'escape'. What does the verb 'escape' suggest about the situation? Explain your answer below.

3 Rewrite each of these sentences using more dramatic verbs.

a The asteroid collided with the planet.

b Pieces of rock flew up after the impact.

c Desperately, she steered out of the way.

Set extension activity

4 Write down as many interesting or dramatic verbs as you can think of to describe each of the things in the boxes below. Some examples have been provided.

Movement	**Speech**
travelling	saying

Sight	**Impact**
looking	bumping

Sound	**Heat**
humming	boiling

Flight	**Fear**
floating	shaking

Verbs and adverbs

5 Underline the adverbs in the following sentences.

a Silently, she crept across the room.
b He hammered frantically on the door.
c "Here we go again," he muttered quietly.
d She glanced sharply at the door.

6 Rewrite the following sentences using adverbs instead of adjectives to describe the action. An example is provided.

His movements were slow.
He moved slowly.

a Her shouts were desperate.

_____

b The collision of the two objects was violent.

_____

c Her grip on the controls was tight.

_____

d His speech was quiet.

_____

7 Rewrite the following sentences removing the adverb and replacing the verb with a more descriptive verb. An example is provided.

She put the folder onto his desk roughly.
She slammed the folder onto his desk.

a She walked quietly across the room.

_____

b When she got to the oxygen tank she was breathing heavily.

_____

c She looked at it intensely.

_____

d She opened it forcefully.

_____

8 Write down as many powerful verbs as you can think of to describe a person's actions when they are angry. For example: *stamped, glared.*

_____

_____

Set extension activity

9 You are going to write a description of the following sequence of events:

- An astronaut is performing some maintenance work on a sealed-off area of a spaceship.
- She realises that the oxygen in this area of the ship is running out quickly.
- She finds that she is trapped.
- She tries to get out.

a Make a list of the feelings the astronaut will experience.

_____

_____

_____

b Write a bank of dramatic verbs that help to convey those feelings.

_____

_____

_____

_____

c Now write two or three paragraphs describing the sequence of events in the bullet points above. Every time you use a verb, pause and think about alternative verbs that may be more descriptive or dramatic.

_____

_____

_____

_____

_____

_____

_____

_____

_____

_____

_____

_____

_____

_____

Section 4
Building noun phrases

In this section, you will practise your skills in building and using noun phrases.

Inferring ideas

1a Look again at the extract on page 106 of the Student Book. Why are the families leaving Earth?

_____

_____

_____

b How does Father feel about leaving Earth?

_____

_____

_____

Exploring noun phrases

2 Look at the following noun phrases. For each one, underline the adjectives and circle the nouns. Then write a sentence explaining what impression the phrase gives of the thing it is describing. An example is provided.

A <u>monstrous, red, boiling</u> (lake.)

The adjectives 'red' and 'boiling' make the lake seem dangerous, while 'monstrous' exaggerates this sense, suggesting that the lake is evil and hostile.

a The tiny, distant, blue dot of a star.

_____

_____

b Its cold, clear, emotionless voice.

_____

_____

c The gut-twisting, muscle-flattening, eye-popping surge of the nuclear engines.

_____

_____

d The warm, friendly, luxurious glow of sunlight on our backs.

_____

_____

Set extension activity

3 Create your own adjective banks in the boxes below. Try to think of as many words as possible that could be used to describe things in each category. Examples are provided.

What something is made of

rocky

Shape

bumpy

Colour

pale

Size

vast

Prepositional phrases

4a Underline the prepositional phrases in the following sentences.

(i) The spaceship was hovering over the crater.
(ii) The asteroid tumbled towards us.
(iii) Behind the panel there was a red button.
(iv) He scuttled across the floor.
(v) The red dust was seeping into the airlock.

b Complete the following sentences using prepositional phrases.

(i) She ran _____ .

(ii) The quadbike sped _____ .

(iii) _____ the dunes stretched on for miles.

Building noun phrases

5a Imagine you have just boarded a spaceship for the first time. It is going to take you and your friends far away from home because the Earth is dying. Write five noun phrases that describe things you see when you enter the spaceship. For example: *rows of sleeping pods.*

_____

_____

_____

_____

_____

b Add appropriate adjectives to each of your noun phrases. For example: *rows of clear glass sleeping pods.*

_____

_____

_____

_____

_____

6 Add a prepositional phrase to each of your noun phrases. For example: *rows of clear glass sleeping pods in the vast dormitory.*

_____

_____

_____

_____

_____

_____

Set extension activity

7 Revise the skills you have covered in the first half of this unit, ready for the assessment in the next lesson. You may find it helpful to note down the key points covered in each of the sections so far. If there are any areas where you do not feel confident, reread the appropriate pages in the Student Book.

Section 1: Creating an impression

You can make an inference about a character based on what the character says or does.

_____

_____

_____

_____

_____

_____

_____

Section 2: Exploring intention and structure

_____

_____

_____

_____

_____

_____

Section 3: Selecting verbs

_____

_____

_____

_____

_____

_____

Section 4: Building noun phrases

_____

_____

_____

_____

_____

Section 5
Assessment

In this section, you will answer questions on a short extract and improve a sample student response.

This extract is from the science fiction novel *The War of the Worlds* by H. G. Wells.

▼ Read the extract and then answer the questions that follow it.

1 When I returned to the common the sun was setting. Scattered groups were hurrying from the direction of Woking, and one or two persons were returning. The crowd about the pit had increased, and stood out black against the lemon yellow of the sky—a couple of hundred people, perhaps. There were raised voices, and some sort of struggle appeared to be going on about the pit. Strange imaginings passed through my mind. As I drew nearer I heard Stent's voice:

5 "Keep back! Keep back!"

A boy came running towards me.

"It's a-movin'," he said to me as he passed; "a-screwin' and a-screwin' out. I don't like it. I'm a-goin' 'ome, I am."

I went on to the crowd. There were really, I should think, two or three hundred people elbowing and jostling one another, the one or two ladies there being by no means the least active.

10 "He's fallen in the pit!" cried some one.

"Keep back!" said several.

The crowd swayed a little, and I elbowed my way through. Every one seemed greatly excited. I heard a peculiar humming sound from the pit.

"I say!" said Ogilvy; "help keep these idiots back. We don't know what's in the **confounded**[1] thing, you know!"

15 I saw a young man, a shop assistant in Woking I believe he was, standing on the cylinder and trying to scramble out of the hole again. The crowd had pushed him in.

The end of the cylinder was being screwed out from within. Nearly two feet of shining screw projected. Somebody blundered against me, and I narrowly missed being **pitched**[2] onto the top of the screw. I turned, and as I did so the screw must have come out, for the lid of the cylinder fell upon the gravel with a ringing **concussion**[3]. I stuck my elbow
20 into the person behind me, and turned my head towards the Thing again. For a moment that circular **cavity**[4] seemed perfectly black. I had the sunset in my eyes.

I think everyone expected to see a man emerge—possibly something a little unlike us **terrestrial**[5] men, but in all essentials a man. I know I did. But, looking, I presently saw something stirring within the shadow: greyish billowy movements, one above another, and then two luminous disks—like eyes. Then something resembling a little grey
25 snake, about the thickness of a walking stick, coiled up out of the writhing middle, and wriggled in the air towards me—and then another.

Key vocabulary

confounded[1]: adds emphasis and expresses annoyance
pitched[2]: pushed or thrown
concussion[3]: violent shock
cavity[4]: hollow space
terrestrial[5]: of the Earth

Assessment questions

1 The narrator meets a boy. What do you infer about the boy's feelings? What gives you this impression?

_____

_____

2 Which two verbs in the following sentence create the impression that the people in the crowd were eager to see what was going on in the pit?

There were really, I should think, two or three hundred people elbowing and jostling one another.

_____

3 What impression do we get of Ogilvy from the way he speaks?

_____

_____

4 Look at the final paragraph. Why does the writer begin a new paragraph at this point?

_____

5 Look at the following question and read the student's response that follows.

Question: How do the descriptions used by the writer create the sense that something very strange is happening?

Response: At first there is a pit in the ground with a cylinder in it, which is very strange, and then it keeps screwing open and then the crowd sees a weird grey thing with eyes. It looks a bit like a snake and everyone is very surprised that it doesn't look like a human.

a What advice would you give to this student to help them improve their response?

_____

_____

_____

_____

_____

b Write your own improved response to the question in the space below. Continue your answer in your notebook.

_____

_____

_____

_____

_____

Section 6
Creating a viewpoint

In this section, you will practise exploring how writers create the narrator's viewpoint in a text.

Intention and viewpoint

1 Look again at the extract on page 112 of the Student Book, then read the following question and sample student answer.

Question: How do Pan's emotions change throughout the extract?

Answer: She starts off quite calm but then gets really scared as more and more things go wrong.

a Rewrite and improve the student's answer. Use quotations from the extract to support your answer.

_____

_____

_____

_____

b How do you think the changes you made improved the student's answer? Explain your answer.

_____

_____

_____

Choosing vocabulary

2 The writer of the extract could have simply written: 'I feel afraid.' Instead they wrote: 'Fear hits the bottom of my stomach like it's been kicked.'

a How do the verbs 'hit' and 'kicked' create a more powerful effect? Explain your answer below.

_____

_____

b Find and write down two more examples of powerful vocabulary choices in the extract that convey the sense of Pan's fear. For each one, explain how the vocabulary creates a powerful effect.

Example 1: _____

_____

Example 2: _____

_____

Set extension activity

3 Plan a piece of writing in which you describe a space traveller experiencing building tension in a moment of crisis. For instance, the spaceship's engines may have overheated and be about to explode.

Make some notes using the prompts below.

a What are the key facts of the situation you have chosen?

_____

_____

_____

_____

_____

b How does the problem get worse and worse in the eyes of the space traveller? How will you order your points to make the tension feel greater and greater?

_____

_____

_____

_____

_____

c Describe any moments of temporary relief that make the character think it's going to be OK after all, before that hope is snatched away.

_____

_____

_____

_____

_____

d Write a list of verbs and phrases that you will be able to use to show the fear the space traveller feels. For example: _my throat was dry; my whole body shook._

_____

_____

_____

_____

_____

Past and present tenses

4 Rewrite the following sentences, changing those which are in the present tense to the past tense, and those which are in the past tense to the present tense.

a Fear gripped my throat and squeezed.

b I'm shaking as I try not to laugh.

c She said she'd rather eat her own arm.

d He stares at me as if I'm a stranger.

e Who did he think he was?

5a The writer of the extract on page 112 of the Student Book has chosen to write in the present tense. In this activity you will be looking at various ways of writing in the past tense. Rewrite paragraphs 2, 3 and 4 of the extract from page 112 of the Student Book (up to and including the first Error message) in the past tense, as if these events have happened a few years ago. Continue your answer in your notebook if needed.

"In the event of an emergency," said the manual,

b Which version (present or past tense) do you feel creates tension more effectively? Explain your answer below.

Set extension activity

6a Write the piece that you planned for **Activity 3** on page 105 of this Workbook, using the first person, present tense. (For example, *I run to the window*). Continue your answer in your notebook if needed.

b Now rewrite what you have written in the past tense. Continue your answer in your notebook if needed.

c Which version do you prefer? Explain your answer below.

This section links to pages 116–119 of the Student Book.

Section 7
Explaining and describing

In this section, you will practise exploring how writers use description in non-fiction texts.

Identifying purpose

1 Look again at the article on page 116 of the Student Book.

a In one sentence, describe the purpose of the opening paragraph.

_____

_____

b Why does the writer use vivid description, rather than detailed explanation, in the opening paragraph?

_____

_____

c In your own words, write an explanation of the benefits of using vivid description to convey some ideas, and clear explanation to convey other ideas.

_____

_____

_____

_____

Structuring an explanation

2 Look again at the concluding paragraph of the article. As the editor, you have been asked to rewrite this paragraph to make it 'appeal to more people'.

a Which detail, mentioned in the concluding paragraph, might be off-putting to some readers? Explain your answer below.

_____

_____

_____

b Rewrite the concluding paragraph so that it appeals to more people.

_____

_____

Set extension activity

3 You are going to write two versions of a description of the same journey. One should convey a positive opinion and create a positive impression of the experience. The other should convey a negative opinion and create a negative impression of the same journey.

a Begin by making notes in the table below, identifying the positive and negative elements of the experience.

Positives	Negatives
the sun was shining	I was too hot

b Now write your descriptions in the space below.

Positive description:

_____

_____

_____

_____

_____

_____

_____

Negative description:

_____

_____

_____

_____

_____

_____

Formal register

4 Rewrite each of the following sentences using a formal register with no contractions.

a The buzz when you take off is awesome!

_____

b Trust me, the Northern Lights will blow your mind.

_____

c You haven't lived until you've experienced zero gravity.

_____

d I'll never forget the experience – it was ace!

_____

Writing an article

5 You have been asked to write a formal article explaining to people who live on Mars what their first holiday to Earth will be like. You will need to describe the journey from Mars to Earth as well as the experience of being on Earth.

a Note down four key facts or statistics that you think readers will find interesting.

_____

_____

_____

_____

b Note down four opinions that you want to convey. For example: _seeing the oceans on Earth is an experience you will never forget._ Continue your answer in your notebook if needed.

_____

_____

_____

_____

c Using the table below, write down as many adjectives as you can think of that you may be able to use in your description of visiting Earth, including the journey to get there.

Sights	Sounds	Other sensations	Emotions	Other
spectacular	thundering	dizzying	frightening	unforgettable

Set extension activity

6 Continue to plan your article about the holiday to Earth that you started in **Activity 5** on the previous page. Plan three paragraphs. For each paragraph, make some notes explaining:

- the key question the paragraph will answer
- how you will present your ideas to engage the reader.

Remember to try to grab the reader's attention with the opening, and end with a surprising or interesting fact or question.

Paragraph 1: _____

_____

_____

_____

Paragraph 2: _____

_____

_____

_____

Paragraph 3: _____

_____

_____

_____

7 Now write your article in the space provided. Remember to use some of the facts, opinions and adjectives you planned in **Activity 5** on the previous page. Continue your answer in your notebook.

_____

_____

_____

_____

_____

_____

_____

_____

_____

This section links to pages 120–123 of the Student Book.

Section 8
Exploring sentence structure

In this section, you will practise exploring different sentence structures in descriptive writing.

Following the camera

1 Using words only (rather than a storyboard), describe what the camera would see in a film of paragraphs 2, 3 and 4 of the extract from page 120 of the Student Book.

Paragraph 2: _____

_____

Paragraph 3: _____

_____

Paragraph 4: _____

_____

Sentence length

2a Find and write down an example from the first paragraph of a short sentence used to highlight a dramatic moment.

_____

b Find and write down an example from the second paragraph of a short sentence used to highlight a key idea.

_____

c Find and write down an example from the fourth paragraph of a longer sentence used to build up descriptive detail.

_____

_____

_____

3 Rewrite the following short sentences as one longer sentence.

It was a lake. It was ringed by tall trees. The trees' lower branches hung down and swept the surface of the water. The water was clear and blue.

_____

_____

Set extension activity

4a Imagine a spaceship spinning out of control. Describe the scene in ten short, simple sentences.

1 _____

2 _____

3 _____

4 _____

5 _____

6 _____

7 _____

8 _____

9 _____

10 _____

b Now rewrite your description as two or three paragraphs. Include some short sentences for impact. Extend several of the sentences to add more descriptive detail or to move events along more smoothly.

_____

_____

_____

_____

_____

_____

_____

_____

_____

_____

_____

_____

_____

_____

_____

_____

_____

_____

Adverbials

5 Underline the adverbials in the sentences below from the extract. Then rewrite each of them, moving the adverbials to a different place in the sentence.

a For a moment, she failed to realise the meaning of the sound.

b Breathlessly, she clambered up the ladder from her cabin.

c Margot ... emerged first, tense and exhausted.

d Suddenly, a cry halted their discussion.

Sentence openings

6 You are going to write a piece describing an abandoned building you have discovered on another planet. Write six short sentences that could form part of that description, two beginning with a noun, two beginning with a pronoun, one beginning with a noun phrase and one beginning with an adverbial.

1

2

3

4

5

6

Planning a description

7a Begin to plan the description you started in **Activity 6**. In one simple sentence, describe how the building looks from the outside.

b Note down everything that the camera would see if filming this scene from outside, looking at the building.

Set extension activity

8a Continue planning your description. Note down what the camera would see as you step inside the abandoned building for the first time.

_____

_____

_____

_____

b Make notes describing your different emotions as you stand outside and then enter the building.

Outside: _____

_____

_____

As you enter: _____

_____

_____

Once you are inside: _____

_____

_____

9 Now write your description in the space below. Try to use varying sentence lengths, and different sentence beginnings, as you have practised in the previous activities.

_____

_____

_____

_____

_____

_____

_____

_____

_____

_____

_____

_____

_____

_____

Section 9
Gathering ideas for a description

In this section, you will practise exploring different ways of planning a description.

Gathering ideas and vocabulary

1 Imagine a scene in which you hear a huge crash just as you are about to walk out of your school's main entrance. You rush outside. There in front of you is huge, round, smoking meteorite. Several smaller meteorites have crashed into the nearby landscape, and when you look into the sky you see more meteorites plummeting towards the Earth.

Using the short description above as a prompt, you are going to plan your own description of the scene and the action that develops from this moment. Note down some ideas about what else you can see in the scene outlined above. For example: *burnt trees, people running away.*

a What can you see right in front of you?

_____

_____

_____

b What can you see further away?

_____

_____

_____

2 Now write ten noun phrases or sentences, each one describing a single detail. Use adverbials and adjectives. For example: *a | burning, blackened | tree | on the ground.*

adjectives   *noun*   *adverbial*

_____

_____

_____

_____

_____

_____

_____

_____

_____

Set extension activity

3 In the space below, draw a sketch of the scene you are planning to describe, including as much detail as possible about the scene and the action. You could also make annotations to describe details.

Gathering ideas – senses

4 For each of the senses below, choose three details from your notes from **Activity 1** on page 116 of this Workbook and describe how they smell, sound or feel. For example: *the blazing tree crackles.* Create new details if necessary.

Smell: _____

_____

Sound: _____

_____

Touch: _____

_____

Gathering ideas – emotions

5 Make some notes detailing the emotions you feel as you take in the scene.

_____

_____

_____

_____

Story structure

6 Complete the table below.

What is the problem or danger you face in this scene?
What events make the danger increase?
How is it resolved?

Set extension activity

7 Look back over the notes you have made for **Activities 1** to **6** on the previous three pages. Make a list of the key details and ideas that you will include to create a tense and engaging description. Remember to think about the basic structure of problem–rising tension–resolution.

_____

_____

_____

_____

_____

_____

_____

_____

_____

_____

_____

_____

_____

8 Now write your description of the scene in the space provided below. Continue your answer in your notebook if needed.

_____

_____

_____

_____

_____

_____

_____

_____

_____

_____

_____

_____

_____

_____

_____

_____

Section 10
Reviewing and revising

In this section, you will further develop your skills of reviewing and improving the choices you have made in your writing.

Reviewing sentence structure and paragraphing

1 Read the following example of a student's descriptive writing.

> The planet was very different to Earth. The ground was covered with purple dust which smelled like matchsticks. There was smoke coming out of holes in the ground. There were strange plants like giant mushrooms. There were three moons in the orange sky. I felt nervous as I stepped outside for the first time. I didn't know whether it was safe. I thought of my family and of home and of what had happened to Earth. I saw some kind of building which was tall and smooth and black after I had walked for about half an hour and I wondered what was inside. Then a door began to open and I hid.

a Write down the first few words of each sentence that should begin a new paragraph.

(i) _____

(ii) _____

(iii) _____

b Rewrite the second, third and fourth sentences as one multi-clause sentence.

_____

_____

_____

c There are four sentences in a row beginning with the pronoun 'I'. Rewrite each of them so that none of them begins with a pronoun.

_____

_____

_____

_____

d The final sentence describes what should be a very dramatic moment. Rewrite and extend it as more than one sentence, including at least one short sentence for impact.

_____

_____

_____

Set extension activity

2a What advice would you give to the student who wrote the description in **Activity 1** on the previous page about how to improve it? Explain your reasons.

_____

_____

_____

_____

_____

_____

b Rewrite the description yourself. You can add more detail if you wish. Remember to vary sentence lengths for effect, and to use a range of sentence beginnings. Continue your answer in your notebook if needed.

_____

_____

_____

_____

_____

_____

_____

_____

_____

c Review what you have written. What steps could you take to improve it further? Remember to check spelling, punctuation and grammar. Write your response as if advising another student, as you did in **Activity 2a**. Continue your answer in your notebook if needed.

_____

_____

_____

_____

_____

_____

_____

_____

Reviewing vocabulary choice

3 The sentences below are taken from a student's description of a scene in which a spaceship is in danger of crashing into the Moon. Rewrite each one, replacing the underlined verbs with more descriptive and dramatic verbs to create a sense of danger.

a "We're not going to make it!" I <u>shouted</u>.

b I <u>held</u> the controls even more tightly.

c For a moment we regained control, then the spaceship <u>dipped</u> suddenly to one side.

d Objects <u>rattled</u> around the cockpit.

Reviewing spelling, punctuation and grammar

4 Read the following text written by a student, which you are going to proofread and rewrite.

> I was tryying realy hard to keep control of the spaceship as it tumbles towards the moon. But watever I did, the spining got faster and faster, I new there was a real danger we would crashed and die. We've only got 30 seconds left to get out of this spin! I shouted I can see the fear on Toms face. The surface of the moon was got closer and closer.

a Underline any examples of incorrectly spelled words and write out the correct spellings here.

b Highlight any examples of verbs in the wrong tense and rewrite them correctly here.

c Circle and correct any examples of incorrect punctuation.

5 Rewrite the text, correcting all the errors.

Set extension activity

6 Revise the skills you have covered in the second half of this unit, ready for the assessment in the next section. You may find it helpful to note down the key points covered in each of the sections so far. If there are any areas where you do not feel confident, reread the appropriate pages in the Student Book. Think back to when you planned for the previous assessment. What helped? What could you improve on?

Section 6: Creating a viewpoint

In a first person viewpoint, the reader sees what the character sees.

Section 7: Explaining and describing

Section 8: Exploring sentence structure

Section 9: Gathering ideas for a description

Section 10: Reviewing and revising

Section 11
Assessment

In this section, you will identify the mistakes in a sample student response and write an improved version.

1 Look at the following task and read the student's response that follows.

> **Task:** Describe a scene in which you arrive for the first time on a planet where you and your companions hope to live permanently.

> **Response:** The door slid open We were amaized. we were on a ridge and we can see for miles. There was forest everywere and there were some rivers and the air smelled sweet and there were no sound. Except for our breething, that feels strange to me. We started walking along the ridge and then we new we was in danger because we herd a loud buzing and then we saw the insects. We were running back to the spaceship and we got there just in time.

You are going to improve and extend this response.

a Underline any spelling or punctuation mistakes.
b Circle any verbs that are in the wrong tense.
c Write a 'V' next to any opportunities to improve the impact of the writing by making different vocabulary choices.
d Write an 'S' next to any opportunities to improve the impact of the writing by varying sentence length and structure.
e Write a 'P' wherever you think paragraph breaks should be added.
f Use the space in the box below to make some notes and plan how you will improve this answer.

2 Write your improved version of the answer in the space below. Remember to:

- create tension
- refer to physical senses in your description
- describe or show the character's feelings and emotions.

This section links to pages 136–139 of the Student Book.

Section 1
Exploring and responding

In this section, you will practise exploring the ways in which poetry can be understood and the effects it can have.

Reading the poem

1 Look again at the poem on page 136 of the Student Book. Write two sentences, one for each stanza of the poem, to explain what you think they are about.

Stanza 1: _____

_____

Stanza 2: _____

_____

Poetry terms

2a Which lines in the poem rhyme?

_____

b How many syllables are there in each stanza?

_____

c Is the rhythm of the first stanza the same as the rhythm of the second stanza?

_____

Exploring key ideas

3a In the simile in the first stanza of the poem, what is being compared to what?

_____

b In your own words, describe how the people in the first stanza make the poet feel.

_____

_____

4a In the simile in the second stanza of the poem, what is being compared to what?

_____

b In your own words, describe how the people in the second stanza make the poet feel.

_____

Set extension activity

5 Create a bank of similes under the following headings. Examples are provided.

a Someone who makes you feel good
Example: *She was like a sparkling light in the gloom.*

_____

_____

_____

_____

_____

b Someone who makes you feel bad or uncomfortable
Example: *His stare was as cold as a glacier.*

_____

_____

_____

_____

_____

c Excitement
Example: *I felt as if my blood was pure adrenaline.*

_____

_____

_____

_____

d Fear
Example: *My stomach churned like a cement-mixer.*

_____

_____

_____

_____

_____

Responding to the poem

6a How does the first stanza make you feel? Include at least one word or phrase from the poem in your response.

_____

_____

b How does the second stanza make you feel? Include at least one word or phrase from the poem in your response.

_____

_____

c Overall, do you feel this is a happy poem or a sad poem? Explain your answer using short quotations from the poem.

_____

_____

_____

_____

Writing a poem

7 You are going to prepare to write a poem expressing how you feel about school.

a Note down some feelings you have about school. For example: _I love seeing my friends; I don't like how tired I feel._

_____

_____

_____

_____

b Pick the four things that you feel most strongly about from your notes in the previous activity and write similes to explain how they make you feel. For example: _I feel as tired as a hibernating bear._

_____

_____

_____

_____

c Note down any words you can think of that rhyme with the final words from each of your similes. For example: _bear = care, share, tear, nightmare._

_____

_____

_____

Set extension activity

8a Write two stanzas of your poem, each with four lines, expressing how you feel about school. Try to use some similes. Use a regular rhythm but without any rhyming.

b Now rewrite the same stanzas, this time using rhyme at the end of some or all lines.

c Decide which of the two versions you prefer, and continue to write your poem with a further two stanzas in the same style.

d Look back over what you have written. How do you think someone who read your poem would imagine that you feel about school?

This section links to pages 140–143 of the Student Book.

Section 2
Responding to ideas

In this section, you will further develop your response to some of the ideas in a poem.

Understanding the poem

1a Read the poem on page 140 of the Student Book. What impression do you get of 'nurse'? Explain your answer below.

_____

_____

_____

b How does the speaker feel about getting married?

_____

_____

_____

c How does the speaker feel about the future she imagines?

_____

_____

_____

Understanding the voice of the poem

2a In one sentence, summarise what you know about the speaker in the poem.

_____

_____

_____

b What do you think is important to the speaker in the poem? Use quotations from the text to support your response.

_____

_____

_____

c Does the speaker seem happy, sad or neither? Explain your answer below.

_____

_____

_____

Set extension activity

3 You are going to write your own poem about the future you imagine for yourself. Make some notes using the following headings as prompts.

a What do you think other people want or expect you to do in the future?

_____

_____

_____

_____

b What might the future look like for you if one or all of those things don't happen?

_____

_____

_____

_____

c Describe what you consider to be a happy future for yourself.

_____

_____

_____

_____

d Now write your poem about your future, beginning with the word 'If'. Try to write at least three stanzas.

_____

_____

_____

_____

_____

_____

_____

_____

_____

_____

_____

_____

_____

Poetry punctuation

4a Look back at the poem you wrote in **Activity 3** on page 131 of this Workbook. Write out one of your stanzas using the correct punctuation you would expect to see if this was not part of a poem.

_____

_____

_____

_____

_____

b Now write it out again, adding capital letters at the beginning of every line, and commas or full stops at the end of every line.

_____

_____

_____

_____

_____

Developing your response

5a Look again at the poem on page 140 of the Student Book. What does the speaker most care about for her future? Explain your answer below, using quotations from the poem.

_____

_____

_____

_____

_____

b What does the poem imply would normally be expected of a young girl about her future? Explain your answer below, using quotations from the poem.

_____

_____

_____

_____

_____

c In what ways do the speaker's ideas about her future differ from or match what is expected of her? Explain your answer below.

_____

_____

_____

_____

Set extension activity

6a What do you think the speaker in the poem on page 140 of the Student Book believes is a woman's role in life? Explain your answer.

_____

_____

_____

_____

b Complete a paragraph beginning with the following statement, using evidence from the poem to support the point.

The poet wrote this poem to express her belief that a woman's role in life is to be a mother, even if she cannot marry.

_____

_____

_____

_____

_____

_____

c Now complete a different paragraph, beginning with this alternative statement:

The poet wrote this poem to show people that women's lives can be restricted by the expectation that they must become mothers.

_____

_____

_____

_____

_____

_____

d Which argument do you most agree with from **6b** and **6c** above, and why?

_____

_____

_____

_____

_____

This section links to pages 144–147 of the Student Book.

Section 3
Responding to a poem

In this section, you will further develop your response to a poem as a whole text.

Exploring meaning

1 Look again at the poem on page 144 of the Student Book. The poet uses metaphors to describe his actions. In your own words, describe what you think the poet means when he says that he:

a 'watered it in fears'

_____

_____

b 'sunned it with smiles'

_____

_____

2 How do you think the poet treats his foe when he uses 'soft deceitful wiles'?

_____

_____

_____

3 Explain whether or not you agree with the following statements.

a The poet regrets allowing his anger to grow.

_____

_____

_____

b The poet pretends not to be angry with his foe.

_____

_____

_____

c The poet is happy to poison his foe.

_____

_____

_____

Set extension activity

4 You are going to write a description of the thoughts, feelings and actions of the foe in the poem, from the day he first noticed the apple growing on the tree to the night when he stole into the speaker's garden. First, make some notes about the foe's feelings during the key stages in the story, under the following headings.

a When the poet uses 'soft deceitful wiles'

_____

_____

_____

b When the foe sees the apple

_____

_____

_____

c When the foe decides to steal into the garden

_____

_____

_____

5 Now write your description of the foe's thoughts, feelings and actions below.

_____

_____

_____

_____

_____

_____

_____

_____

_____

_____

_____

_____

_____

_____

_____

Conjunctions

6 Rewrite the following pairs of sentences, linking them with conjunctions so that each pair becomes one longer sentence.

a He was my foe. I did not tell him that I was angry.

_____

b He wanted the apple. He knew it was mine.

_____

c He crept into the garden. He wanted the apple.

_____

d The apple killed him. It was poisonous.

_____

Responding to the poem

7a Did the foe deserve what happened to him? Explain your answer below using quotations from the poem.

_____

_____

_____

_____

_____

b Do you feel as if you are on the speaker's side? Explain your answer below using quotations from the poem.

_____

_____

_____

_____

_____

c What do you think the poet wants the reader to understand? Explain your answer below.

_____

_____

_____

_____

_____

Set extension activity

8 You are going to write a poem about taking your revenge by deliberately getting someone else into trouble. It does not need to be true. Make some notes using the following questions as prompts.

a What did they do to make you want to take revenge?

_____

_____

_____

b What were your thoughts and feelings about their actions?

_____

_____

_____

c How did you get them into trouble?

_____

_____

_____

d What were your thoughts and feelings when you saw your plan had worked?

_____

_____

_____

e What metaphor could you use for your feelings of revenge, like the metaphor of the poisoned tree in the poem on page 144 of the Student Book?

_____

_____

_____

9 Now write your poem in the space below. Continue your answer in your notebook if needed.

_____

_____

_____

_____

_____

_____

_____

_____

Section 4
Selecting evidence

In this section, you will practise responding to the viewpoint expressed in a poem and select evidence from the poem to support your response.

Retrieving information

1a Look again at the poem on page 148 of the Student Book. List three things that the speaker's sister likes to do.

_____

_____

_____

b Who uses these items? Write 'Speaker' or 'Sister' next to each of the following:

sword _____

torch _____

pen _____

fishing rod _____

Inferring ideas

2 Look at the following adjectives:

imaginative | courageous | clever | adventurous | active | cautious

Write two sentences about the speaker, using one or more of the adjectives. Include quotations from the poem to show why you feel they describe the character.

_____

_____

_____

_____

3 'The speaker thinks that her sister is better than her'. Do you agree or disagree with this statement? Explain your answer below.

_____

_____

_____

_____

Set extension activity

4 You are going to write a diary entry, as if you are the speaker from the poem on page 148 of the Student Book. Your diary entry should describe a family holiday. Focus on describing the sister and your feelings about her. Make some notes using the following questions as prompts.

a As the speaker, what do you think and feel about your sister, generally?

_____

_____

_____

_____

b What did your sister do while you were on holiday together?

_____

_____

_____

_____

c How did you feel when your sister was doing these things?

_____

_____

_____

_____

5 Now write your diary entry in the space provided below. Continue your answer in your notebook if needed.

_____

_____

_____

_____

_____

_____

_____

_____

_____

_____

_____

_____

_____

Punctuating quotations

6 The sentences below all use quotations from the poem on page 148 of the Student Book; however, speech marks have not been used. Rewrite the sentences, adding speech marks where appropriate.

a Although her sister laughs at my fears, the speaker is happy to be the one with the torchlight.

b The speaker describes her sister wielding a makeshift sword.

c The speaker feels the stories she reads will leave their spark.

Using evidence

7a Select and note down three quotations from the poem that give you a strong impression of the personality of the speaker's sister.

b Underline the one quotation selected for **Activity 7a** that gives the strongest sense of her personality.

c Write a sentence or two in which you make a statement about the sister's personality, backed up with the quotation you have chosen from the poem.

Writing a response

8 Write a response to the following question: What impression do you get of the way the speaker feels about her sister in the poem? Remember to:

- make a statement about your impression
- support your statement(s) with relevant quotations from the poem
- explain how the quotation created the impression you have described.

Continue your answer in your notebook if needed.

Set extension activity

9 Revise the skills you have covered in the first half of this unit, ready for the assessment in the next section. You may find it helpful to note down the key points covered in each of the sections so far. If there are any areas where you do not feel confident, reread the appropriate pages in the Student Book.

Section 1: Exploring and responding

Sentences in poetry often continue over more than one line.

Section 2: Responding to ideas

Section 3: Responding to a poem

Section 4: Selecting evidence

This section links to pages 152–153 of the Student Book.

Section 5
Assessment

In this section, you will answer questions on a poem and improve a sample student response.

▼ **Read the poem and then answer the questions that follow it.**

The Chimney Sweeper
by William Blake

(Note: This poem was published in 1789 at a time when it was common for young boys to be made to work as chimney sweeps – work which was extremely dangerous and often resulted in loss of life.)

1 When my mother died I was very young,
   And my father sold me while yet my tongue
   Could scarcely cry "weep! weep! weep! weep!"
   So your chimneys I sweep & in soot I sleep.

5 There's little Tom Dacre, who cried when his head
   That curled like a lamb's back, was shaved, so I said,
   "Hush, Tom! never mind it, for when your head's bare,
   You know that the soot cannot spoil your white hair."

   And so he was quiet, & that very night,
10 As Tom was a-sleeping he had such a sight!
   That thousands of sweepers, Dick, Joe, Ned, & Jack,
   Were all of them locked up in coffins of black;

   And by came an Angel who had a bright key,
   And he opened the coffins & set them all free;
15 Then down a green plain, leaping, laughing they run,
   And wash in a river and shine in the Sun.

   Then naked & white, all their bags left behind,
   They rise upon clouds, and sport in the wind.
   And the Angel told Tom, if he'd be a good boy,
20 He'd have God for his father & never want joy.

   And so Tom awoke; and we rose in the dark
   And got with our bags & our brushes to work.
   Though the morning was cold, Tom was happy & warm;
   So if all do their duty, they need not fear harm.

Assessment questions

1 Do the stanzas in this poem have a regular rhythm?

2 In the third stanza, what is used as a metaphor for chimneys?

3 What evidence can you find in the poem that the speaker is kind?

_____

_____

4 Read these two statements:

A The poet believes that if chimney sweeps get on with their work without complaining, they will come to no harm.

B The poet believes that chimney sweeps have a miserable existence and should fear for their lives.

Which statement do you most agree with? Write a few sentences to explain your answer.

_____

_____

_____

_____

_____

5 Look at the following question and read the student's response that follows.

Question: How does this poem make you feel?

Response: At first the poem is about a boy who is sold by his father as a chimney sweep. There is another boy Tom Dacre who is quite sad sometimes but the speaker cheers him up and then he has a dream about playing by a river and it is all OK.

a What advice would you give to this student to help them improve their response?

_____

_____

_____

_____

b Write your own improved response to the question in the space below. Continue your answer in your notebook.

_____

_____

_____

_____

_____

_____

_____

Section 6
Exploring vocabulary

In this section, you will practise exploring the poet's vocabulary choices and experiment with your own.

Exploring the poem

1 Look again at the poem on page 154 of the Student Book. Rewrite the poem as a conversation (or argument), writing down only dialogue (words that are spoken). Continue your answer in your notebook if needed. For example:

"Calm down."

"No!"

Responding to the poem

2a How do you imagine the person being addressed in the poem feels as the scene progresses? Write one or two sentences explaining your ideas.

b What parts of the poem helped you to imagine that?

3a What are your impressions of the person being addressed in the poem?

b How has the poet created that impression? Choose one quotation from the poem and use it to support your answer.

Set extension activity

4 Look back at what you wrote for **Activity 1** on page 144. You are going to rewrite the scene, still including dialogue but also adding in description to help convey thoughts, feelings and setting. Try to convey all the emotions that the poem suggests for each of the characters. For example:

I could see she was cross as soon as she came into the living room.

"Calm down," she said, gritting her teeth as she noticed what I'd written on the wall.

"No!" I yelled back at her. "And you can't make me!"

_____

_____

_____

_____

_____

_____

_____

_____

_____

_____

_____

_____

_____

_____

_____

_____

_____

_____

_____

_____

_____

_____

_____

_____

Set extension activity

_____

Apostrophes of possession

5 Rewrite the following sentences using an apostrophe to show possession. An example is provided.

The pens belong to Amy.
They are Amy's pens.

a The name of the woman is Rupal.

_____

b The games belonging to the boys are in the other room.

_____

c The goal scored by Nanda was the best.

_____

d Bedtime for Hau is 8:00 p.m.

_____

Responding to vocabulary choices

6a Look again at the fourth stanza of the poem on page 154 of the Student Book. Write down two words or phrases that sound playful.

_____

b Why do you think the poet chose these words? Write a sentence or two explaining your answer, including the words or phrases in your answer.

_____

_____

_____

Experimenting with vocabulary choices

7 You are going to prepare to write a poem in which you are being asked by an adult to do something. It could be tidying up, reading a book, doing homework, putting your clothes away, all of those things, or other similar things. You are not in the mood for any of it. Make some notes outlining who is asking you to do what, and why you don't want to do it. Try to include some words and phrases that convey the tone of voice of each character.

_____

_____

_____

_____

Set extension activity

8 Continue gathering vocabulary ideas for the poem you began to plan in **Activity 7**. Note down any words or phrases that you think would powerfully convey the right emotions under the following headings.

a Physical actions:

b Facial expressions:

c Anger:

9 Now write your poem, using the most powerful vocabulary you have identified. You could choose to begin your poem in the same way as the one on page 154 of the Student Book: *If you...*

Section 7
Exploring figurative language

In this section, you will practise exploring the poet's use of figurative language, and the effects this can create.

Understanding figurative language

1 Look at the following phrases. Some are metaphors and some are similes. Write 'metaphor' or 'simile' next to each one to indicate which it is. Then rewrite the similes as metaphors, and vice versa. An example is provided.

Her eyes were shining like gemstones. (simile)   *Her eyes were gemstones. (metaphor)*

a The tentacles of jealousy.

_____

b Rays of hope warmed me.

_____

c My phone is a true friend.

_____

d The building was as confusing as a rabbit warren.

_____

2 Look again at the poem on page 158 of the Student Book. Write down the metaphor that you feel most powerfully suggests positive feelings about the phone, and the metaphor that most powerfully suggests negative feelings.

Positive: _____

Negative: _____

3 Write two or three sentences explaining how the poet has used figurative language (metaphors in this case) to show how the speaker's relationship with the phone changes. Use the metaphors you selected in the previous activity to support your statements.

_____

_____

_____

_____

Set extension activity

4 Create four of your own metaphors under each of the headings below. Examples are provided.

a Technology
Example: *My computer was my jailer.*

_____

_____

_____

_____

b Home
Example: *We burrowed into our den.*

_____

_____

_____

_____

c Friendship
Example: *We were two puppies play-fighting.*

_____

_____

_____

_____

d School
Example: *The new student was a bison — all muscle and brute force.*

_____

_____

_____

_____

e Love
Example: *Love is a warm blanket.*

_____

_____

_____

_____

Similes and clichés

5 Rewrite the following over-used similes (clichés) with new images to create new, imaginative comparisons.

a as hard as nails

_____

b as dull as dishwater

_____

c as pretty as a picture

_____

d as quick as a flash

_____

Experimenting with figurative language

6 You are going to prepare to write a poem about winning a competition. You were excited about winning the huge cash prize. Then, as time goes by, your feelings about the money change.

a Make some notes about how the money might become a problem. For example: _All my friends were jealous and nobody spoke to me anymore._

_____

_____

_____

_____

b Think about how you feel after winning the money. Write down three more similes or metaphors, creating positive comparisons with the money. For example: _The money was my future. The money was freedom._

_____

_____

_____

_____

c Now think about how the money might start to become a problem. Write down three more similes or metaphors to help create this sense. For example: _The money was an ugly smirk on my friends' faces._

_____

_____

_____

_____

Set extension activity

7a Write the poem you planned for in **Activity 6** on the previous page, using metaphors and/or similes to show how your feelings about winning the money change over time. Continue your answer in your notebook if needed.

b Look back over what you have written. In the space below, rewrite all the similes you have used as metaphors, and all the metaphors as similes.

c Do you think metaphors or similes are more powerful? Explain your answer below.

Section 8
Exploring form

In this section, you will practise looking at how poets shape poetry.

Look back at the poem 'The Chimney Sweeper' on page 142 of this Workbook and answer the following questions.

Reading the poem

1a Who is the speaker? How would you describe him?

_____

_____

b How does the speaker comfort Tom Dacre?

_____

_____

c What does Tom dream of that night?

_____

_____

Exploring the poet's ideas

2a Note down all the words and phrases that create a positive, happy image in the dream.

_____

_____

b Why do you think the poet uses so much positive language in the lines describing the dream?

_____

_____

_____

c The poem finishes 'So if all do their duty, they need not fear harm.' What do you think the poet means by this?

_____

_____

_____

Set extension activity

3 Look again at the poem 'Nettles' on page 162 of the Student Book. Plan your own prose description of a real or imagined accident or incident involving a young child. Make some notes using the following questions as prompts.

a What happened?

_____

_____

_____

_____

b How did the child feel and react?

_____

_____

_____

_____

_____

c How did the parents feel and react?

_____

_____

_____

_____

_____

4 Now write your description in the space provided.

_____

_____

_____

_____

_____

_____

_____

_____

_____

_____

_____

_____

Rhyme

5 Read the two versions of the third stanza from 'The Chimney Sweeper' below: the version on the left is from the original poem, and the version on the right has had one word changed.

And so he was quiet, & that very night, As Tom was a-sleeping he had such a sight! That thousands of sweepers, Dick, Joe, Ned, & Jack, Were all of them locked up in coffins of black;	And so he was quiet, & that very night, As Tom was a-sleeping he had such a dream! That thousands of sweepers, Dick, Jack, Ned, & Joe, Were all of them locked up in coffins of black;

a Which version sounds younger and more playful? Why is this?

_____

b Why do you think the poet chose to write 'The Chimney Sweeper' using regular rhyme?

_____

_____

Punctuation

6 Read this stanza from 'The Chimney Sweeper'.

There's little Tom Dacre, who cried when his head
That curled like a lamb's back, was shaved, so I said,
"Hush, Tom! never mind it, for when your head's bare,
You know that the soot cannot spoil your white hair."

a How many sentences are there in the stanza above?

_____

b Rewrite the stanza, breaking it up into three sentences.

_____

_____

_____

_____

Form

7 'The Chimney Sweeper' uses a regular rhythm that repeats through the stanzas, which are all of equal length. Look again at the poem 'Nettles' on page 162 of the Student Book, which includes one stanza only and a range of line-lengths. Why might the poet who wrote 'Nettles' have chosen not to use a regular rhythm and line-length? Think about what is being described in the poem as you explain your answer below.

_____

_____

_____

Set extension activity

8 Rewrite the poem, 'Nettles', from page 162 of the Student Book. In your new version, try to include:

- more than one stanza
- a regular rhythm
- similar line-lengths throughout.

Nettles

_____

_____

_____

_____

_____

_____

_____

_____

_____

_____

_____

_____

_____

_____

_____

_____

_____

_____

_____

_____

_____

_____

9 Read the original and your new version aloud. How does your version change the feel of the poem? Explain your answer below.

_____

_____

_____

_____

_____

This section links to pages 166–169 of the Student Book.

Section 9
Exploring structure

In this section, you will practise exploring the form and structure of a poem and then write your own.

Verbs and nouns

1 The poem on page 166 of the Student Book uses a lot of nouns derived from verbs, for example 'sadness stealer'. Turn each of the following descriptions into a noun. An example is provided.

Example: *Someone who wakes you up in the middle of the night =* sleep wrecker

a Someone who invades your privacy

_____

b Someone who interrupts your phone calls

_____

c Someone who spoils your fun

_____

Exploring ideas

2 Make a list of all the things the speaker describes his mother doing.

_____

_____

_____

_____

_____

_____

3 Using the notes you have made, write a paragraph answering the following question: How does the speaker feel about his mother? Remember to use quotations from the text.

_____

_____

_____

_____

_____

_____

_____

_____

Set extension activity

4 Imagine you are the speaker from the poem on page 166 of the Student Book. Using the ideas in the poem, you are going to write a prose description of the speaker's mother, from the perspective of the speaker.

a Plan your writing by identifying two or three headings, each covering one type of thing that the speaker's mother does that (as the speaker) you like. Note down all of the relevant things that the speaker's mother does under each heading.

b Now write your description of the speaker's mother in the space provided below, using the ideas you have gathered in the previous activities.

Pronouns and repetition

5 Rewrite the passage below, using pronouns to avoid repetition.

My mother is amazing. My mother looks after us all when we're ill. My mother's bedtime stories are brilliant. My brother and I fight over who gets to sit on my mother's lap but my brother and I always think that my mother is fair.

Exploring form

6 Look again at the final stanza of the poem on page 166 of the Student Book:

> She's my
> Never glum,
> Constant chum
> Second to none
> We're under her thumb!
> Mum!

a How many syllables are there in each of the first five lines?

Line 1: _____

Line 2: _____

Line 3: _____

Line 4: _____

Line 5: _____

b How do the line lengths change from line 1 to line 5?

c What is the effect of this development in the number of syllables? Think about how they set the tone for the final line of the stanza.

d Why do you think the poet chose to end the poem with the single word 'Mum!'? Explain your answer below.

Set extension activity

7 You are going to write a poem about your home, including the people in it. You could write only positive things, or a mixture of positive and negative.

a How does your home make you feel? Try to use only one or two words for each feeling.

_____

_____

_____

_____

_____

b How do the people you share your home with make you feel and what do they do to make you feel this way?

Action (what someone does)	How that makes you feel

c Do any of the ideas you have made notes about sit together well in pairs, either because they are linked in meaning or because they rhyme, or sound appealing in another way when paired? Note down any such pairs here:

_____

_____

_____

_____

d Now write your poem in the space provided. Continue your answer in your notebook if needed.

_____

_____

_____

_____

_____

_____

_____

_____

_____

Section 10
Comparing poems

In this section, you will practise comparing the features and effects of two different poems.

Planning a comparison

1 You are going to compare two poems that you have already explored:

- 'Bookworm' by Jill Carter (on page 148 of the Student Book)
- 'Mum' by Andrew Peters (on page 166 of the Student Book)

Reread both poems.

a Make some notes in the tables below, including quotations from the poem to back up your observations.

How does the speaker feel about the person they are describing?	
'Bookworm'	**'Mum'**

What do we learn about the speaker?	
'Bookworm'	**'Mum'**

b Note down any key similarities or differences between the two poems based on your notes in the tables above. Continue your answer in your notebook if needed.

Set extension activity

2 You are going to continue planning for a comparison of the poems 'Bookworm' and 'Mum' that you started in **Activity 1** on the previous page.

a Make some notes in the tables below, including quotations from the poems to back up your observations.

What choices have the poets made about the form of their poems?	
'Bookworm'	**'Mum'**

What interesting vocabulary choices have the poets made?	
'Bookworm'	**'Mum'**

b Note down any key similarities or differences between the two poems based on your notes in the tables above.

Writing a comparison

3 Write your comparison of the two poems in the space below. Remember to:

- Explore similarities.
- Explore differences.
- Discuss choices the poets have made.
- Give examples from the poems.

Set extension activity

4 Revise the skills you have covered in the second half of this unit, ready for the assessment in the next lesson. You may find it helpful to note down the key points covered in each of the sections so far. If there are any areas where you do not feel confident, reread the appropriate pages in the Student Book. Think back to when you planned for the previous assessment. What helped? What could you improve on?

Section 6: Exploring vocabulary

Adding an apostrophe and the letter 's' to a noun can show possession.

_____

_____

_____

_____

Section 7: Exploring figurative language

_____

_____

_____

_____

_____

Section 8: Exploring form

_____

_____

_____

_____

_____

Section 9: Exploring structure

_____

_____

_____

_____

_____

Section 10: Comparing poems

_____

_____

_____

_____

Section 11
Assessment

In this section, you will identify the mistakes in a sample student response and write an improved version.

▼ **Read the poem and then answer the questions that follow it.**

The sick child

by Robert Louis Stevenson

1 CHILD.
O Mother, lay your hand on my brow!
O mother, mother, where am I now?
Why is the room so **gaunt**[1] and great?
5 Why am I lying awake so late?

MOTHER.
Fear not at all: the night is still.
Nothing is here that means you ill -
Nothing but lamps the whole town through,
10 And never a child awake but you.

CHILD.
Mother, mother, speak low in my ear,
Some of the things are so great and near,
Some are so small and far away,
15 I have a fear that I cannot say,
What have I done, and what do I fear,
And why are you crying, mother dear?

MOTHER.
Out in the city, sounds begin
20 Thank the kind God, the carts come in!
An hour or two more, and God is so kind,
The day shall be blue in the window-blind,
Then shall my child go sweetly asleep,
And dream of the birds and the hills of sheep.

> ### Key vocabulary
> **gaunt**[1]: miserable in appearance

1 Look at the following question and sample student response.

> **Question:** How does the poet convey the emotions of the characters in this poem?

> **Response:** This poem was about a mother an a child talking to each other in the nite. The child is sic and seemed quiet scarred like things are trying to get him and the mother trys to look after him. But he didnt know were he is or what he is scarred of and he is very confused because the room seemed strange. The mother is upset because her child is sic and she told him not to be scarred and she prays for morning to come so that the child can go to sleep.

You are going to improve and extend this response.

a Underline any spelling or punctuation mistakes.

b Circle any verbs that are in the wrong tense.

c Write a 'V' next to any opportunities to improve the impact of the writing by making different vocabulary choices.

d Write an 'S' next to any opportunities to improve the impact of the writing by varying sentence length and structure.

e Use the space in the box below to make some notes and plan how you will improve and extend this answer.

2 Write your improved version of the answer in the space below. Continue your answer in your notebook if needed. Remember to:

- address the question of how the poet conveys the characters' emotions
- use quotations from the poem to back up points made
- describe how we learn about each character from what they say and from what the other says to them
- write at least three paragraphs.

This section links to pages 178–181 of the Student Book.

Section 1
Describing

In this section, you will practise exploring how writers craft descriptions to achieve their intention.

Comprehension

1 Look again at the extract on page 178 of the Student Book and answer the following questions.

a Who watches the narrator eat?

_____

b What food items are mentioned as part of the meal?

_____

c Where does the narrator go after eating?

_____

Identifying the writer's intention

2 Underline the most suitable word from the options in the sentences below. Underneath each sentence, write down a quotation from the extract to support your chosen options.

a The narrator finds it funny/difficult/easy/annoying to eat the food.

_____

b The narrator wants to please/annoy/disobey/challenge his father.

_____

c His father does not want the narrator to worry/argue/relax/speak.

_____

3 What impression do you get of the relationship between the narrator and his father? How has the writer given this impression?

a Note down a few quotations that show how the narrator behaves towards or thinks about his father.

_____

_____

_____

b Note down a few quotations that show how the father behaves towards or thinks about his son.

_____

_____

_____

Set extension activity

4a In the box below, create a word bank of 20–30 adjectives to describe food both positively and negatively.

Positive adjectives	Negative adjectives
tasty	bitter

b Choose your favourite four words from each column, and use each one in a sentence describing different foods.

(i) _____

(ii) _____

(iii) _____

(iv) _____

(v) _____

(vi) _____

(vii) _____

(viii) _____

Comma splices

5a The following sentence contains a comma splice. Rewrite it correctly as two sentences.

I hated him, I stared at the floor.

_____

b The following sentence contains a comma splice. Rewrite it correctly, replacing the comma with a conjunction.

The mouse was annoyed, the cat was excited.

_____

c Two of the following sentences contain comma splices and are grammatically incorrect. Place a cross next to the sentences that are incorrect.

A I thought about something else, trying not to vomit.   ☐

B Looking at it carefully she could see it was some kind of writing, it was a diary!   ☐

C Tomorrow will be awful, at least I only have to do it once.   ☐

Now write correct versions of the sentences you have marked as incorrect, using a full stop or a conjunction.

_____

_____

Selecting vocabulary

6 You are going to write a description of eating a meal where the food and atmosphere are both horrible. Look back at the word bank of negative adjectives describing food that you created on the previous page. Now complete the table below, creating a similar list of words that might be used to describe the location of the meal, the person or people you are eating with, and the mood.

Location	People	Mood
suffocating	scowling	angry

Set extension activity

7a Using the vocabulary you produced for **Activity 6** on the previous page, write two paragraphs describing the horrible meal. Remember to use adjectives to create a negative impression of the meal. Think about all of your senses, and about how you and the other people feel.

b Rewrite the two paragraphs you have written for **Activity 7a**, making as few changes as possible but turning it from wholly negative to wholly positive.

Section 2
Persuading

In this section, you will practise exploring a persuasive text and its structure, and then write your own.

Facts and opinions

1 Look again at the extract on page 182 of the Student Book. Identify one fact and one opinion from each of the four paragraphs.

Paragraph 1	Fact: _____
	Opinion: _____
Paragraph 2	Fact: _____
	Opinion: _____
Paragraph 3	Fact: _____
	Opinion: _____
Paragraph 4	Fact: _____
	Opinion: _____

Inference

2a Look at the following two sentences. The writer has not stated their opinion clearly. What idea or opinion can you infer from each sentence?

(i) I've met people who say that until they started running every day, they felt too tired to get out of bed every morning.

_____

_____

(ii) Of course running might feel like hard work, but nobody ever improved their fitness by sitting on the sofa!

_____

_____

b The following is a clear statement of opinion. Rewrite it so that the opinion is not stated explicitly but must be inferred by the reader.

Playing computer games is bad for your health.

_____

Set extension activity

3 The extract on page 182 of the Student Book tries to persuade the reader to learn how to cook. Plan to write a similar text persuading people to do more exercise. In a later activity you will use these notes to write your own article.

a Note down four or five facts about exercise that might persuade people to do more exercise.

b Note down four or five key positive opinions about exercise.

c Now write a sentence for each opinion given in **Activity 3b**. Do not state your opinion explicitly, but write it in a way that means the reader can infer your opinion.

Apostrophes in contractions

4 Rewrite the following sentences using contractions. Remember to use an apostrophe.

a I have never believed in hard work.

_____

b You will never know until you try.

_____

c She could not have made it more obvious.

_____

d Climbing that mountain will be the hardest thing I will ever do.

_____

e Who is going to stop me?

_____

Structure

5a Look at the following pairs of sentences. Which would work best as opening sentences? Which would work best as final 'call to action' sentences? In the boxes, write '1' for the opening sentence or '2' for the final sentence.

A   Raising money for a charity is one of the most rewarding things you'll ever do.   ☐

    Sign up today!   ☐

B   Let's clean up our act.   ☐

    We are all responsible for the natural environment.   ☐

C   Find the time to be still.   ☐

    Meditation is a great way to relax and clear the mind.   ☐

b Look again at the notes you made in **Activity 3** on the previous page for an article to persuade people to do more exercise. Write an opening sentence for the article that introduces the topic and states your opinion about it.

_____

_____

c Write a closing sentence for the article that speaks directly to the reader with a call to action.

_____

_____

d Now choose the three key benefits of doing more exercise that you think will be most persuasive to readers and write them below.

_____

_____

_____

Set extension activity

6a Write your article persuading people to do more exercise. Aim to write three or four paragraphs. Remember to include:

- contractions for a more informal tone
- a clear opening sentence to introduce the topic and your opinion
- a benefit, your opinion about it and a related call to action in each paragraph
- a final call to action that inspires the reader to do more exercise.

_____

_____

_____

_____

_____

_____

_____

_____

_____

_____

_____

_____

_____

_____

_____

_____

_____

_____

_____

_____

_____

_____

_____

_____

_____

_____

_____

_____

_____

_____

b Read through your article carefully. Make any improvements where you find opportunities to make the tone more informal, or to address the reader directly.

Section 3
Vocabulary choice

In this section, you will practise exploring the writer's choice of vocabulary in a descriptive text and then try writing your own.

Finding and inferring key information

1 Look again at the extract on page 186 of the Student Book and answer the following questions.

a Where did the writer's family live before they moved to London?

_____

b What was the first thing the writer's aunt gave him to taste?

_____

c Which three spices does the writer mention?

_____

d What will be the writer's most important dish at his new restaurant?

_____

Using adjectives

2a Underline the adjectives in each of the following phrases from the extract.

   (i) and the mouth-watering aromas of garlic, cinnamon and peppercorns
  (ii) Our first feast was a fiery sweet curry with Thai steamed rice
 (iii) lightly salted, and perfectly fragrant with lemon grass, ginger and basil

b Rewrite the following sentences, adding just one adjective to each sentence to make a more powerful and positive description.

  (i) The cake was covered with cream.

_____

 (ii) The smell of bread filled the air.

_____

(iii) Finally, she drizzled honey over her creation.

_____

3 In one paragraph, write a positive description of some food that someone once cooked for you. Use a few carefully chosen adjectives to make the experience seem as wonderful as possible.

_____

_____

_____

_____

_____

Set extension activity

4a In the box below, make a list of positive adjectives that could be used to describe food. Try to use adjectives that link to as many senses as possible, not just to taste.

sizzling

b Write ten sentences about food you have eaten, using some of the adjectives you have listed in **Activity 4a** to make the food sound appealing. An example is provided.

My favourite food is pizza, straight out of the oven with the cheese still sizzling.

(i)

(ii)

(iii)

(iv)

(v)

(vi)

(vii)

(viii)

(ix)

(x)

Nouns

5a Underline the plural nouns in this list. Rewrite the singular nouns as plural nouns.

sweet   _____

desserts   _____

flavours   _____

recipe   _____

herbs   _____

b Write 'C' for 'concrete' or 'A' for 'abstract' next to each of these to indicate which type of noun it is.

taste-buds   _____

joy   _____

memory   _____

mouth   _____

satisfaction   _____

Writing a description

6a Imagine that someone has cooked you the most disgusting breakfast imaginable. You sit down at the table but the food is not ready yet. Make some notes about what you can see, smell and hear in the room.

_____

_____

_____

_____

_____

_____

_____

_____

b Now your breakfast has been placed in front of you. Make some more notes about how it looks, smells and tastes. Try to use detailed nouns and negative adjectives in your notes. For example: _slimy, undercooked egg-white dribbles..._

_____

_____

_____

_____

_____

_____

Set extension activity

7 You are going to write a description of the disgusting breakfast you started planning in **Activity 6** on the previous page. Look back at the notes you made to help you.

a Write three paragraphs. The first should describe the setting (the room). The second should describe the moment the food arrives. In the third you should describe eating the food. Remember to think about all of your senses and to describe how the experience makes you feel. Use specific nouns and carefully chosen adjectives.

b Look back over what you have written and check for any opportunities to add details that will help the reader to understand what you experienced.

Section 4
Persuasive vocabulary

In this section, you will practise exploring the writer's choice of vocabulary in a persuasive text and then try writing your own.

Writers' intentions

1 Look at the following extracts taken from the webpage on page 190 of the Student Book. Explain how each extract works as a way of persuading the reader to visit the restaurant.

a Many of our customers have been eating with us for years – and now they bring their children, and even their grandchildren!

_____

_____

b the finest recipes to create a menu to appeal to everyone.

_____

_____

c succulent seafood, tender chicken, crisp vegetables, sizzling stir-fries

_____

_____

d our friendly, helpful staff are waiting to create a memorable meal for you.

_____

_____

e Just five minutes from Central Station

_____

_____

2 Find a quotation to support each of the following statements about the webpage.

a The writer wants you to know that the food is of a very high standard.

_____

b The writer wants the restaurant to appeal to a wide range of people who may want different things from the experience.

_____

c The writer wants you to believe that the restaurant's atmosphere is welcoming.

_____

Set extension activity

3a Imagine you have been hired to write the homepage text for a local restaurant's website. In note form, write three or four points to persuade people to visit the restaurant under each of the headings below.

History

1 _____

2 _____

3 _____

4 _____

Location

1 _____

2 _____

3 _____

4 _____

Food

1 _____

2 _____

3 _____

4 _____

Atmosphere

1 _____

2 _____

3 _____

4 _____

b Look back through what you have written and for each heading underline the one point which you think is the most persuasive.

c In no more than two sentences, summarise the four persuasive points you have underlined.

_____

_____

_____

_____

Noun phrases

4 Write a noun phrase based on each of the following nouns to give more descriptive detail.

a sandwich _____

b room _____

c bowlful _____

d cake _____

e restaurant _____

Vocabulary choices

5 Underline the superlatives in the sentences below.

A The race tomorrow will be the longest I have run.
B Who has made the tastiest jam?
C That was the best, most exciting film I have ever seen!

6a Underline the example of alliteration in the sentence below.

The broken machine clicked and clacked clumsily.

b Now write your own example of alliteration in a sentence, describing either something you ate yesterday or how you ate it.

_____

_____

_____

7a Look back at the four points you identified as the most persuasive in **Activity 3** on the previous page. Rewrite one of them using at least one superlative.

_____

_____

_____

b Rewrite another of the persuasive points using alliteration.

_____

_____

_____

c Rewrite the final two of the four points using noun phrases to add to the description.

_____

_____

_____

_____

Set extension activity

8 Revise the skills you have covered in the first half of this unit, ready for the assessment in the next lesson. You may find it helpful to note down the key points covered in each of the sections so far. If there are any areas where you do not feel confident, reread the appropriate pages in the Student Book.

Section 1: Describing

A comma splice is the incorrect use of a comma to link two separate clauses.

Section 2: Persuading

Section 3: Vocabulary choice

Section 4: Persuasive vocabulary

This section links to pages 194–195 of the Student Book.

Section 5
Assessment

In this section, you will answer questions on a short text and improve a sample student response.

▼ **Read the extract and then answer the questions that follow it.**

The Tasty Classroom Summer Camp

1   Come along to The Tasty Classroom for a summer camp that will change your life!

2   Here at the Tasty Classroom we've been teaching young people how to cook for thirty years. And even though we've grown into the biggest and best-loved cookery school in the country, we're still true to the same principle we started out with. The best teachers make lessons FUN!

Learn new skills

3   Try your hand at making tongue-tingling ice cream, gorgeous, gooey cakes, savoury dishes to die for and much, much more. Whatever your skill level, we'll show you how to perfect the cooking techniques you'll be wowing your friends and family with for years to come.

Make new friends

4   Most people who come to our summer camps say it's the friends they make that keep them coming back year after year. There's something about cooking a delicious meal together, and then eating it together, that just brings people – well – together! In fact, two of the teachers here met on a summer camp when they were young, and they've been best friends ever since!

Get creative

5   Weights and measurements, temperatures and timings are really important in cooking, but the most important ingredient is something else entirely: creativity. Sign up for our summer camp and you'll get the chance to come up with more wild and crazy ideas for cooking than Willy Wonka!

Cook better, eat better, live better

6   Not that we're all about sweets of course! Here you'll also learn how to use the freshest, best ingredients so that your cooking doesn't just taste mouth-wateringly yummy but helps you look after a healthy body and mind too. Sounds too good to be true? It isn't. You just need to learn how to do it.

7   So sign up today for a fun-filled summer of cooking you'll never forget!

Assessment questions

1 What is the overall purpose of this extract? What is the writer trying to persuade the reader to do?

_____

2 Write down an example of a superlative from the second paragraph of the extract.

_____

3 In the second paragraph, which sentence is intended to persuade you that attending the summer camp is a positive experience?

4 Write down three adjectives from the third paragraph that make the food sound appealing.

5 What is the key point in the fourth paragraph?

6 Look at the following question and read the student's response that follows.

Question: How does the writer try to persuade the reader to attend the summer camp?

Response: The writer says you should come on the summer camp because you can learn how to cook lots of nice things and it is a really really good school where the teachers are fun so you will have a really good time and get to make really tasty ice cream and other things like cakes. The writer says you shouldn't just eat sweets though because you need to be healthy which is really important and you'll probably make some new friends as well.

a What advice would you give to this student to help them improve their response?

b Write your own improved response to the question in the space below.

Section 6
Structuring persuasive writing

In this section, you will practise exploring the structure of a persuasive text, and craft some persuasive writing of your own.

Imperative verbs

1 Place a tick next to each of the sentences below that includes an imperative verb.

A Eat less, do more! ☐

B Lots of snacks are bad for you. ☐

C Don't eat in between meals. ☐

D Do your own research into healthy eating. ☐

2a Look again at the extract on page 196 of the Student Book. Rewrite the subheadings so that they do not include imperative verbs. Try to use a variety of alternatives to the verb 'eat'.

_____

_____

_____

_____

_____

b Do your rewritten subheadings make the extract more or less effective? Explain your answer.

_____

_____

Paragraphs and structure

3 Look at the text below. Rewrite it, splitting it into two paragraphs and giving each a subheading that includes an imperative verb. Continue your answer in your notebook if needed.

It is well known that spending too much time inside can be bad for your health. Try to get outside for at least one hour every day and you will soon feel the benefits. Think about ways to include time spent outside as part of your daily routine. Research shows that people who walk or cycle for part of their journey to school spend twice as much time outside as others.

_____

_____

_____

_____

Set extension activity

4 Write a plan for what you would include in a longer leaflet about the benefits of spending more time outdoors. You could think about mental and emotional benefits as well as physical ones. Plan what you would include in five paragraphs. Give each paragraph a subheading with an imperative verb and outline the key point you would make in each paragraph.

Paragraph 1

Subheading: _____

Key point

_____

_____

Paragraph 2

Subheading: _____

Key point

_____

_____

Paragraph 3

Subheading: _____

Key point

_____

_____

Paragraph 4

Subheading: _____

Key point

_____

_____

Paragraph 5

Subheading: _____

Key point

_____

_____

Quotations

5 Rewrite each of these sentences, adding the correct punctuation.

a It'll all be better in the morning said Mum.

_____

b I wish I believed that was true! Amy replied.

_____

c Mum thought for a minute. Then she said I've got an idea.

_____

Structuring persuasive paragraphs

6 Summarise the first three paragraphs in the extract on page 196 of the Student Book. For each paragraph, note down what it tells you to do and why it says you should do it.

Paragraph 1

What? _____

Why? _____

Paragraph 2

What? _____

Why? _____

Paragraph 3

What? _____

Why? _____

7 Look back at **Activity 4** on the previous page of this Workbook. Write up the first paragraph from your persuasive leaflet plan. Remember to:

- tell the reader to do something
- explain why they should do it
- refer to evidence if possible.

_____

_____

_____

_____

_____

_____

Set extension activity

8a Complete your persuasive leaflet arguing that people should spend more time outside. Give the leaflet a heading, then for each paragraph include a key point or instruction and back each point up with a reason. Try to include some quotations from experts. These could be real or made up.

_____

_____

_____

_____

_____

_____

_____

_____

_____

_____

_____

_____

_____

_____

_____

_____

_____

_____

_____

_____

_____

_____

_____

_____

_____

_____

_____

_____

_____

b Look back over what you have written. Check that you have correctly punctuated any sentences that include quotations.

This section links to pages 200–203 of the Student Book.

Section 7
Structuring persuasive sentences

In this section, you will practise exploring how sentences can be structured in different ways to make meaning clear or to make a point more persuasive.

Short instructions with longer explanations

1a Look again at the article on page 200 of the Student Book. The writer makes their points in seven short paragraphs. For each paragraph, note down whether the instruction is positive ('Do'), negative ('Don't') or both.

(i) _____   **(ii)** _____   **(iii)** _____

(iv) _____   **(v)** _____   **(vi)** _____

(vii) _____

b The writer could have organised the points differently, starting with all the positive points, then moving on to the negative ones. Would structuring the points that way have been more or less persuasive? Explain your answer.

_____

_____

_____

2a Rewrite the following sentences, dividing each into two sentences so that one is a short instruction and the other a longer explanation. Change some of the words if necessary.

(i) Don't let your dog eat chocolate because dogs have extremely sensitive stomachs and chocolate can make them very unwell.

_____

_____

(ii) Try to keep your cats indoors when you move to a new house because they can take a while to accept a new home and if you let them out too soon they may run away to look for the home they are familiar with.

_____

_____

_____

b Write down the word at the beginning of each of your two 'explanation' sentences in i) and ii) from **Activity 2a**. Next to each, write a label, for example 'verb'/'noun'/'pronoun', to identify the type of word it is.

(i) _____

(ii) _____

Set extension activity

3 Write ten short sentences giving instructions using imperative verbs. After each one, add a longer sentence explaining why the instruction is important. An example is provided. Your ten instructions do not need to link to each other – they can be on different topics.

Example: *Do not try this at home! Fire-eating can be very dangerous and unless practised by trained professionals can cause serious injury.*

Varying sentence length

4 Each of the following includes more than one instruction on the same topic. Rewrite each point, linking the sentences together with conjunctions to form one longer sentence.

a Feed your cat nutritious food. Don't let them eat your leftovers.

b Allow your cat to explore their outside environment. Let them come back inside when they want to.

c Play with your cat. They need mental stimulation. This encourages them to be social.

Using dashes and semi-colons

5 Rewrite these sentences with two clauses, replacing the conjunctions with a semi-colon or a dash.

a Cats are great fun and you can play with them all the time!

b Don't let your cat near expensive furniture as they might scratch it.

c Cats have good reflexes so they are great at landing on their feet.

Varying sentence structure

6a Write your own point with two clauses about looking after a pet. Use a semi-colon or dash rather than a conjunction to link the clauses.

b Now write a second point, this time using conjunctions to combine two or three clauses into one sentence.

c Finally, write a third point with a short instruction sentence followed by a longer explanation sentence.

Set extension activity

7a Choose a topic, such as how to live a healthy lifestyle, and write a persuasive leaflet including six tips. Some tips should advise people what to do. Others should advise them what not to do. Each point should include an instruction and an explanation. Try to vary the way that you present your points, in particular the explanations, using the range of sentence structures that you have practised.

Title: _____

_____

_____

_____

_____

_____

_____

_____

_____

_____

_____

_____

_____

_____

_____

_____

_____

_____

_____

_____

_____

_____

_____

_____

b Look back at what you have written. Check that you have:

- used imperative verbs in the instruction sentences
- included explanations for each instruction
- used a range of sentence structures.

Section 8
Rhetorical devices

In this section, you will practise exploring how writers use language devices to make their ideas more persuasive.

Identifying the writer's point of view

1 Look again at the text on page 204 of the Student Book. Write a one-sentence summary of the main point made in each paragraph.

a _____

_____

b _____

_____

c _____

_____

d _____

_____

Rhetorical devices

2 Look at the quotations below, taken from the text on page 204 of the Student Book. Underneath each one, indicate which rhetorical device is being used. Choose from the following:

- rhetorical question
- direct address
- repetition
- emotive language.

a   What are the most important lessons we need to learn in our lives?

_____

b   we are preparing our children for short lives, with minds and bodies starved of the fuel they need.

_____

c   They will never experience the satisfaction of producing something that everyone sitting together around a table can enjoy.

_____

d   how to grow food, how to keep it fresh, how to cook with real ingredients and how to create real food

_____

e   If your children are being taught anything less than this,

_____

Set extension activity

3 Find one or more articles either online or in a newspaper that use rhetorical devices. Note down four examples of each rhetorical device in the boxes below.

Rhetorical questions
1
2
3
4

Direct address
1
2
3
4

Repetition
1
2
3
4

Emotive language
1
2
3
4

Using colons

4a Rewrite these sentences, combining them into one sentence using a colon.

(i) Every day the weather is the same. Grey, wet and cold.

(ii) Cats are amazing. They're so clever!

b Write your own sentence listing some elements of good weather, using a colon.

c Write your own sentence about a pet or hobby, using a colon to link the clauses.

Using rhetorical devices

5 Rewrite these sentences as rhetorical questions.

a You may never have seen anything so exciting.

b Food has never looked this good.

6 Rewrite these sentences using direct address.

a I always make time to cook using proper, fresh ingredients.

b Do people read the ingredients on food packaging carefully?

7a Write a sentence about drinking fewer sugary drinks using emotive language. For example, you might mention a dramatically unpleasant effect of drinking sugary drinks.

b Rewrite your sentence so that it is also presented as a rhetorical question.

c Write a final sentence, warning people not to drink sugary drinks, using repetition.

Set extension activity

8a Write a persuasive article arguing that people should drink fewer sugary drinks. Remember to:

- begin a new paragraph each time you move on to a new point
- use lots of emotive language
- include some rhetorical questions
- address the reader directly
- include some instances of repetition if possible
- aim to write at least three paragraphs.

b Look back over what you have written and try to find opportunities to add or improve your rhetorical devices.

Section 9
Leaflets

In this section, you will practise exploring the key features of a persuasive leaflet.

Informal tone

1 Rewrite the points below using a more formal tone, suitable for a business hotel's website.

a There's a chilled vibe so you can take it easy at the end of a packed day.

_____

b We've got a great place with big rooms, soft beds and awesome hot showers!

_____

2 Rewrite the sentences below in a more informal tone, suitable for a takeaway restaurant leaflet.

a We select the freshest, finest ingredients to create wonderfully satisfying meals.

_____

b Once you have sampled our food, you will return repeatedly.

_____

3 Explain why a formal tone is more suited to a business hotel's website than to a fish and chips leaflet.

_____

_____

_____

Lists

4 Which of the following would best be presented as a numbered list? Which would best be presented as a bulleted list? Copy each item into the correct column in the table below.

Travel directions | Recipe | Packing list for a holiday | List of events planned for the day | Instructions for making a chair | Shopping list

Numbered list	Bulleted list

Set extension activity

5a Write a short guide explaining how to produce and lay out a persuasive leaflet. Include:

- the purpose of leaflets
- the key features of leaflets
- the type of language usually found in leaflets
- examples to illustrate your points.

For example: *A subheading may be used to introduce a section of the leaflet. Subheadings may use positive vocabulary or imperative verbs, e.g. Shop with us for the freshest local ingredients!*

b Check back over what you have written. Are there any opportunities to use numbered or bulleted lists? If so, update your guide.

Planning a leaflet

6a You are going to plan a leaflet advertising a theme park. Make notes on the following:

Theme park name	Theme park logo
List of key attractions (e.g. rides, cafes)	
Some special offer ideas	
Adjectives that will persuade people to visit your theme park (e.g. 'thrilling')	

b Write a sentence advertising your best special offer idea. Use an imperative verb and at least one of the persuasive adjectives you have listed.

c Write a description of one of the rides, using emotive language and a rhetorical question to explain why people will love it. For example: *Ride our rollercoaster, The Death Swoop, for the biggest thrill of your life. Are you brave enough?*

d Write a description of another ride, this time using either repetition or alliteration along with one or more of the adjectives you noted in the table above.

Set extension activity

7 Create your leaflet for a theme park on this page. Remember to include:

- the name of the theme park
- a logo
- a heading
- a list of features of the theme park, such as rides
- a special offer.

Look for opportunities to add:

- emotive language
- rhetorical questions
- alliteration
- repetition

- direct address
- imperative verbs
- varied sentence structure
- numbered or bulleted lists.

Section 10
Reviewing, revising and proofreading

In this section, you will practise checking and improving the accuracy and effectiveness of a student's persuasive leaflet.

Reviewing spelling, punctuation and grammar

1 Read this leaflet, produced by students at First Choice Academy to advertise a carnival in their town. Circle any errors of spelling, punctuation and grammar you can find in the text.

ITS A GOOD DAY OUT!

You can play the best games, you can enjoy the rides and amusements. You can listn to some great music.

Weve got the best food and drink. Curies and salads. Juices are four sale and tea. You will also enjoy the cakes.

You can do some shopping and buy the best clothe, jewelerry and art. You will find lots of things that you like!

Reviewing vocabulary and sentence structure

2 Look at the food items listed in the leaflet. For each one, write an adjective you could use to describe them in a way that will make people want to taste them.

kebabs _____   curries _____

salads _____   juices _____

tea _____   cakes _____

3a Write an 'S' next to each of the words below that is a superlative.

most brilliant _____   loveliest _____

great _____   freezing _____

super _____   delicious _____

tastiest _____   super _____

b Rewrite these two sentences from the leaflet using more dramatic superlatives.

(i) You can play the best games.

_____

(ii) Weve got the best food and drink.

_____

Set extension activity

4a Soon you will complete an assessment in which you will be asked to write a leaflet advertising a shop that sells food. Use the left-hand column to write a list of as many adjectives as you can think of that could be used to describe food. In the right-hand column, write down all the superlatives you can think of to describe food. These could be superlative versions of the adjectives you list, or they could be entirely different.

Adjectives	Superlatives
fantastic	crispiest

b Look back through your adjectives and try to create five examples of alliteration by adding nouns to the adjectives. For example: *fantastic fries*.

Adding rhetorical devices

5a Rewrite the following words, adding an adjective before each noun and using repetition. You need not write a grammatically correct full sentence.

juices, teas and cakes

_____

_____

b Rewrite the following sentence as a rhetorical question.

You must be ready for a fantastic day out.

_____

Word families

6 Write the adverb forms of the following adjectives. An example is provided.

Adjective	Adverb
clever	cleverly
delicious	
quick	
convenient	
colourful	
gentle	

Checking for comma splices

7 Look for an example of a comma splice in the leaflet advertising the carnival on page 200 of this Workbook. Rewrite it below as two correct sentences.

_____

_____

Checking for apostrophes in contractions

8a Rewrite these words using apostrophes of contraction. An example is provided.

Uncontracted	Contracted
you are	you're
I will	
they have	
did not	
you had	
he is	

b There are two examples of missing apostrophes of contraction in the leaflet advertising the carnival on page 200 of this Workbook. Rewrite them below with the apostrophe inserted in the correct place.

_____

Set extension activity

9 Revise the skills you have covered in the second half of this unit, ready for the assessment in the next section. You may find it helpful to note down the key points covered in each of the sections so far. If there are any areas where you do not feel confident, reread the appropriate pages in the Student Book. Think back to when you planned for the previous assessment. What helped? What could you improve on?

Section 6: Structuring persuasive writing

Imperative verbs give the reader a command or instruction, such as 'sit down'.

Section 7: Structuring persuasive sentences

Section 8: Rhetorical devices

Section 9: Leaflets

Section 10: Reviewing, revising and proofreading

Section 11
Assessment

In this section, you will identify the mistakes in a sample student response and write an improved version.

1 Look at the following task and read the student's response that follows.

Task: Create a leaflet advertising a cake shop.

Response:

CAKES AND BISCUITS FOR SALE

We made lot's of cakes and lot's of biscits. We hoped you want to try them.

We make birthday cakes and gingerbread and weding cakes, lot's of other kinds of cakes. Our bakers are the best. Whatever you want, weve got it. Weve got the best ingredients.

You should come to our cake shop, its the best cake shop in town.

Special offer: buy one of our tastey cakes and get five biscits as well.

You are going to improve this response.
a Underline any spelling or punctuation mistakes.
b Circle any verbs that are in the wrong tense.
c Write a 'V' next to any opportunities to improve the impact of the writing by making different vocabulary choices.
d Write an 'S' next to any opportunities to improve the impact of the writing by varying sentence length and structure.
e Write an 'R' next to any opportunities to add rhetorical devices.
f Use the space in the box below to make some notes and plan how you will improve this answer.

2 Write your improved version of the answer in the space below. Remember to include:

- a logo
- a heading
- the main text for the leaflet
- a special offer.

This section links to pages 220–223 of the Student Book.

Section 1
Exploring key features

In this section, you will practise exploring the key features of instruction texts and their purposes.

Understanding the text

1 Look again at the webpage on page 220 of the Student Book. Circle T or F to indicate which of the statements below are true or false.

A Einstein discovered gravity when an apple fell on his head. [T / F]

B Jules Verne was an early astronaut. [T / F]

C Rockets were first used in China. [T / F]

D Rockets are light so that it is easier to propel them into orbit. [T / F]

E Rockets must travel at 280 km/h in order to enter orbit. [T / F]

2 Identify two types of technology that have been proposed as alternatives to rockets carrying fuel in order to propel them into orbit.

_____

_____

Summarising key information

3 Write down the most important piece of information contained in each paragraph of the first section of the webpage ('The first rockets').

a _____

b _____

c _____

d _____

4 Write your own short summary of the second section of the webpage, 'How does a rocket work?'.

_____

_____

Set extension activity

5 Identify a topic that you would like to write an information text about. For example, this could be a sport, hobby or subject that you're interested in. Note down at least eight interesting facts that you would include in your text. Continue your answer in your notebook if needed.

Topic: _____

1 _____

2 _____

3 _____

4 _____

5 _____

6 _____

7 _____

8 _____

Key features of information texts

6 Look back at the webpage on page 220 of the Student Book.

a Write down an example from paragraph 1 that gives an historical explanation.

_____

b Write down an example from paragraph 3 that uses a familiar example.

_____

c Write down an example from paragraph 4 that explains a purpose.

_____

d Write down an example from paragraph 5 that explains a key idea.

_____

7 In information texts, why are events commonly listed in chronological order? Write your answer below.

_____

_____

Planning an information text

8 Look back at the notes you made in **Activity 5** on the previous page.

a Extend one of the points to explain a key idea.

_____

_____

b Extend one of the points to explain a purpose.

_____

_____

c Extend one of the points using a familiar example.

_____

_____

_____

d Extend one of the points by providing statistics.

_____

_____

Set extension activity

9 Write an information text on the topic you have written notes about in **Activities 5** and **8**.
Remember to list events in chronological order where relevant, and where possible to include:

- subheadings
- explanations of key ideas
- explanations of purpose
- familiar examples
- explanations of history
- statistics.

Section 2
Exploring an instruction text

In this section, you will practise exploring some of the key features of instruction texts and write your own.

Features and structure of instruction texts

1 Draw lines linking each feature listed below to its most appropriate use.

Features	Uses
heading	contains one key point
subheading	gives a visual explanation of something
diagram	identifies the subject of the text
paragraph	outlines a sequence in a particular order
bullet point	identifies the topic of a section of text
numbered list	presents a list but not a sequence

2 Write a short explanation of the difference in purpose between using a numbered list and a bulleted list.

_____

_____

_____

3a Number these points from 1 to 5 to show the order in which they should appear in an instruction text.

A State the process for completing the task. ☐

B Explain the concept. ☐

C State what items are needed. ☐

D Introduce the topic. ☐

E Highlight something important to remember. ☐

b What is the overall purpose of all instruction texts?

_____

_____

Set extension activity

4a You have been asked to write an instruction text explaining 'How to write an instruction text'. Write your text in the space below and remember to include:

- an explanation of the concept and purpose
- a list and explanation of the key features
- a list of steps to complete
- a key point to remember.

Do not include subheadings.

_____

_____

_____

_____

_____

_____

_____

_____

_____

_____

_____

_____

_____

_____

_____

_____

_____

_____

_____

b Look back over what you have written. Would the text be more effective if you included subheadings? Explain your answer below.

_____

_____

_____

_____

Evaluating an instruction text

A girl was asked to write an instruction text explaining to a neighbour how to look after her pet cat while she was away on holiday. Read what she wrote below:

My cat
1 Feed her.
2 Check that her water bowl is full every morning.
3 Be nice to her.
4 She sometimes runs away.

5 What do you think the girl needs to do to make her instruction text more effective? Write three tips below.

_____

_____

_____

_____

_____

6 Rewrite the text yourself, adding in any extra information or structural features that you think are needed.

_____

_____

_____

_____

_____

_____

_____

_____

Adverbials for sequencing

7 Rewrite the following list of instructions explaining how to get to school by bus as five sentences. Start each sentence using an adverbial.

1 Check you have your bus pass.
2 Walk to the end of the road and wait for the bus.
3 Wave at the bus so that the driver knows to stop.
4 Tell the driver the name of the school you are going to.
5 Get off the bus outside your school.

_____

_____

_____

_____

Set extension activity

8 Create your own adventure challenge, including drawing a map and writing instructions on how to complete the challenge. The challenge could be to search for a lost city, a mission to reach enemy headquarters, or anything else you can think of!

Remember to explain everything clearly so that the reader knows exactly what they have to do. Include:

- an introduction explaining why someone should follow your instructions
- a list of things the reader will need in order to complete the challenge
- instructions for the reader to follow in order to complete the challenge
- any important warnings that will keep the reader safe.

Think about whether to use adverbials, numbers or bullets. Continue in your notebook if needed.

MAP

INSTRUCTIONS

This section links to pages 228–231 of the Student Book.

Section 3
Organising information

In this section, you will practise exploring how information can be structured.

Finding information

1 Look at the text on page 228 of the Student Book and answer the following questions.

a What is the most famous thing about the dodo?

_____

b Why is it unlikely that humans hunted the dodo for food?

_____

c Why are paintings of dodos unlikely to be accurate?

_____

d Why did most of the stuffed dodo in Oxford have to be thrown away?

_____

Structuring information

2 Look at the following points about the Great Fire of London. Each pair of points would be included in a single paragraph. Think of a suitable subheading for each paragraph.

a Subheading: _____

 (i) The Great Fire of London happened in 1666.
 (ii) The fire began in a bakery.

b Subheading: _____

 (i) Before the fire, a drought in London had made the city very dry.
 (ii) In 1666, lots of people had houses made from wood which burned easily.

c Subheading: _____

 (i) We know what happened because people wrote about it in newspapers and diaries.
 (ii) Artists also painted pictures of the fire afterwards.

d Subheading: _____

 (i) People whose homes had burned down lived in tents while buildings were rebuilt.
 (ii) A lot of the rebuilt houses were made of bricks instead of wood.

3 Why is it a good idea to include subheadings in information texts? Explain your answer below.

_____

_____

_____

Set extension activity

4 Research an extinct animal of your choice using the internet or other sources. Note down ten facts about the animal and then organise these facts under three different subheadings in the boxes below.

Subheading: _____

Facts:

_____

_____

_____

_____

_____

_____

Subheading: _____

Facts:

_____

_____

_____

_____

_____

_____

Subheading: _____

Facts:

_____

_____

_____

_____

_____

Information and intention

5 Look at the following question and sample answer about the text on page 228 of the Student Book.

Question: What or who does the writer blame for the extinction of the dodo?

Answer: *The writer blames animals and rats for the extinction of the dodo.*

The answer is not wrong, but it does not give a complete picture. Add a second sentence to more fully explain the writer's view.

Planning an information text

6 You are going to plan to write your own information text about an animal that is not extinct yet but is in danger of becoming extinct, such as the polar bear.

a Note down ten facts about your chosen animal. Continue your answer in your notebook if needed.

b Write down three or four suitable subheadings for each paragraph and decide how you will group your points under each heading. Think about whether or not you will follow a chronological structure.

c Decide what order the paragraphs should appear in. You can number the subheadings and points you selected in **Activity 6b**.

d Make some brief notes about what effect you want to have on the reader other than just presenting them with information. For example: *I want to shock people into action; I want to make people feel...*

Set extension activity

7 Write your information text about an animal that is in danger of becoming extinct, using the plan that you made on the previous page.

Remember to:

- include subheadings
- think about how you will achieve the effect that you want the text to have on the reader.

Section 4
Choosing precise vocabulary

In this section, you will practise selecting vocabulary to convey information as clearly and precisely as possible.

Informing and describing

1 Rewrite the instructions below on how to light a fire, making them clearer by adding at least one adjective or adverb to each one. You could choose some of the ideas below, or use your own ideas.

unattended | short | dry | carefully | thicker | gently | neat | conical | small

A Gather grass and twigs, sticks and logs.

B Place the grass and twigs in a pile.

C Light the grass and twigs with matches or a lighter.

D After a few minutes, add one or two logs.

E Do not leave the fire.

Formal and informal registers

2a Rewrite each of the instructions from **Activity 1** using an informal tone to make the process sound fun and easy to learn.

A

B

C

D

E

b Would you use the formal or informal version in a leaflet with the title *Safety First: Important information for your outdoor challenge*? Explain your answer below.

Set extension activity

3a Look again at the juggling instructions on page 232 of the Student Book. Follow them and try to learn to juggle yourself, using scrunched up balls of paper.

Note down any of the instructions that are not clear now that you have tried to follow them. Rewrite them to make them even clearer.

_____

_____

_____

_____

_____

_____

_____

_____

_____

_____

_____

_____

_____

_____

_____

_____

_____

_____

_____

_____

_____

_____

_____

_____

_____

_____

_____

b Look back at the information you have written. Could you make your meaning clearer by adding any adjectives or adverbs? Have you included any adjectives or adverbs that do not make it easier for readers to understand the instructions? Make any improvements you can identify.

Tense and person

4 Rewrite the following sentences in the simple present tense, second person plural. An example is provided.

I lit the fire.   *You light the fire.*

a We drove past the big red sign.   _____

b They had been waiting for five minutes. _____

c You are using oven gloves.   _____

d I was making a note of the time.   _____

e He has put the fire out carefully.   _____

Writing clearly and precisely

5a Rewrite the following instruction, removing any unnecessary adjectives and adverbs.

Pour icy, cold water on the burning fire to put it out but be careful of the billowing clouds of hissing steam that may rise from the red-hot fire when you do this.

_____

_____

b Rewrite the following instruction, removing any unnecessary details.

When the fire begins to die down, add more logs. Now is a great time to sit back and have a cup of tea. Place the logs on the fire carefully so that they do not cause the fire to spread.

_____

_____

c Rewrite the following instruction, using an imperative verb.

It's a good idea to keep any blankets or other flammable items a short distance from the fire.

_____

_____

6 Which of the following are accurate tips for somebody planning to write a set of instructions? Tick those that are accurate. Place a cross next to those that are not.

A Add adjectives that make the instructions more specific.   ☐

B Add adverbs to make the text sound livelier.   ☐

C Remove any unnecessary descriptive words.   ☐

D Place the instructions in the same order in which they should be completed. ☐

E Make sure you include everything the reader will need to know to complete the task. ☐

F If you think something is very obvious, you don't need to mention it.   ☐

G You must use a formal register.   ☐

Set extension activity

7a Write a clear and simple set of instructions explaining how to play a simple game of your choice, such as a card game.

_____

_____

_____

_____

_____

_____

_____

_____

_____

_____

_____

_____

_____

_____

_____

_____

_____

_____

_____

_____

_____

_____

_____

_____

_____

_____

_____

b Look back at what you have written and make any necessary improvements. Think about whether:

- any informative or descriptive words should be added or removed
- the tone should be more or less formal
- the tense and person are appropriate for instructions
- points are numbered where appropriate to indicate the correct order in which steps should be followed.

This section links to pages 236–239 of the Student Book.

Section 5
Writing clearly

In this section, you will practise structuring sentences to convey information as clearly and precisely as possible.

Combining key points

1 Look again at the extract on page 236 of the Student Book and answer the following questions.

a Write down two facts about the game *Spacewar!*

_____

_____

b What is the connection between The Odyssey and the Atari consoles?

_____

_____

Sentence structure

2 Rewrite each of the following multi-clause sentences from the extract as two single-clause sentences.

a It was a version of the pen-and-paper game noughts and crosses, also known as tic-tac-toe.

_____

b It was first known as The Brown Box, but was later renamed The Odyssey.

_____

3 Rewrite each of these pairs of sentences from the extract as one multi-clause sentence.

a Video games are a massive part of many of our lives. Research suggests that young people in some parts of the world spend more time playing video games than watching television or playing sport.

_____

_____

_____

b Four years later, Steve Russell of the Massachusetts Institute of Technology created *Spacewar!* This was a battle game played by two players, each controlling a spaceship circling a planet.

_____

_____

_____

Set extension activity

4a Write eight sentences about a topic of your choice: four single-clause sentences and four multi-clause sentences. The multi-clause sentences should feature a variety of conjunctions.

_____

_____

_____

_____

_____

_____

_____

_____

_____

_____

_____

_____

_____

b Rewrite the multi-clause sentences as pairs of single-clause sentences. In each case, write down which version you prefer, giving reasons.

_____

_____

Preference: _____

_____

_____

Preference: _____

_____

_____

Preference: _____

_____

_____

Preference: _____

_____

Varying sentence structure

5 You are going to plan and write a short informative article about riding a bike safely.

a Write five single-clause sentences about riding a bike, each with a subject-verb opening. For example: *Some people ride bikes to school or work.*

(i) _____

(ii) _____

(iii) _____

(iv) _____

(v) _____

b Note down any other key points you would like to make about riding a bike safely. Each point should be made using a single-clause sentence.

_____

_____

_____

_____

_____

6 Pick two pairs of sentences from **Activity 5** that link together, and combine them into two multi-clause sentences.

a _____

_____

b _____

_____

7 Write at least two paragraphs on the subject of riding a bike safely. Try to use a variety of single-clause and multi-clause sentences. Continue your answer in your notebook.

_____

_____

_____

_____

_____

_____

_____

Set extension activity

8 Revise the skills you have covered in the first half of this unit, ready for the assessment in the next lesson. You may find it helpful to note down the key points covered in each of the sections so far. If there are any areas where you do not feel confident, reread the appropriate pages in the Student Book.

Section 1: Exploring key features

In order to write a summary, firstly identify the key points of information.

_____

_____

_____

_____

Section 2: Exploring an instruction text

_____

_____

_____

_____

_____

Section 3: Organising information

_____

_____

_____

_____

_____

Section 4: Choosing precise vocabulary

_____

_____

_____

_____

_____

Section 5: Writing clearly

_____

_____

_____

_____

Section 6
Assessment

In this section, you will answer questions on a short extract and improve a sample student response.

▼ **Read the extract and then answer the questions that follow it.**

Tarantulas

1 Tarantulas are the stuff of living, scuttling nightmares to some people. These huge, hairy spiders – the biggest in the world – regularly feature in horror stories as the ultimate symbol of terror. In fact, although the bite of a tarantula is painful, they are largely harmless to humans. Including their legs, these giant spiders can grow to nearly 30 cm across, making them around the same size as a large birthday cake. However their venom is less strong than that of a bee.

Hunting

6 Tarantulas are carnivores. They feast mainly on insects, and sometimes also on small vertebrates such as frogs, lizards, mice and small birds. They don't catch their prey in webs. Instead, they ambush their victims and bite them, paralyzing them by injecting venom through their fangs. The tarantula's fangs also deliver enzymes that slowly turn their victims' bodies into liquid that the spider can then suck up and digest.

Hunted

10 The pepsis wasp specialises in attacking tarantulas. It is a gruesome process. The wasp detects the tarantula using its powerful sense of smell, stings the spider and then lays eggs in its paralysed body. When the eggs hatch, the baby wasps eat the tarantula alive.

Reproduction

The male tarantula spins a web, depositing sperm as it does so. He then makes a swift exit if possible – female tarantulas are known to eat males. The female then wraps the male sperm along with her own eggs in a cocoon and
15 guards it for two months, after which up to 1,000 baby tarantulas may hatch.

Assessment questions

1 Which of the following statements are true and which are false? Circle T or F for each one.

A Tarantulas are the most poisonous spiders in the world. [T / F]

B Tarantulas are not the biggest spiders in the world. [T / F]

C Tarantulas sometimes eat birds. [T / F]

D Everyone is afraid of tarantulas. [T / F]

E Female tarantulas sometimes eat males. [T / F]

F Tarantulas catch wasps in their webs. [T / F]

2 Look at the opening sentence of the extract. Which word reveals the writer's intention to grab the reader's attention?

3 Place a tick next to the statement below that most accurately describes the writer's intention.

A The writer wants us to understand that tarantulas are terrifying.   ☐

B The writer wants us to understand that tarantulas are not terrifying.   ☐

C The writer wants us to understand more about tarantulas.   ☐

4 Write down two examples of statistics from the extract.

_____

_____

5 Write down one example of a single-clause sentence from the second paragraph of the extract.

_____

6 Look at the following question and read the student's response that follows.

Question: The writer wants to present information about tarantulas in an interesting and engaging way. How effectively has the writer achieved this?

Response: Tarantulas can be very, very scary hairy and can be as big as a cake but really even though their bite can hurt they are not that dangerous for people and wasps can kill them. It was interesting to read about how they kill their food and don't use a web to catch them. 1,000 baby spiders is a lot!

a What advice would you give to this student to help them improve their response?

_____

_____

_____

_____

_____

b Write your own improved response to the question in the space below. Continue your answer in your notebook if needed.

_____

_____

_____

_____

_____

_____

_____

_____

Section 7
Paragraphing information

In this section, you will practise exploring how to structure paragraphs of information.

Topic sentences

1 Read these pairs of sentences that appear at the beginning of paragraphs. For each pair, underline the topic sentence.

a The Andes contain some of the most challenging mountains in the world. Anyone wanting to climb them must be very fit and strong.

b You can be the best climber in the world, but your foot can still slip. Climbing can be extremely dangerous.

Responding to the text

2 Read the following paragraph and answer the questions.

Joe had been hanging in mid-air for a long time and Simon was beginning to lose his grip. Eventually, Simon realised that if he was to survive, he had to cut the rope and let Joe die. Tears well up in Simon's eyes when he recalls the moment – it is every climber's worst nightmare. At the time though, arms weak, trembling with cold and his boots beginning to slip down the side of the mountain after holding Joe for an age, Simon made the decision very quickly.

a Write down the topic sentence.

_____

_____

b What impression does the writer want to give of Simon? Is he a coward? A villain? A hero who has done all he can? Explain your answer below.

_____

_____

_____

c How has the writer created this impression?

_____

_____

_____

_____

Set extension activity

3 You have been asked to write a guide to your school for some new students who are joining next term. Write eight subheadings that could appear in the guide, and then write the topic sentence that would appear in a paragraph beneath each subheading.

Heading: **A guide to your new school**

Subheading: _____

Topic sentence: _____

_____

Subheading: _____

Topic sentence: _____

_____

Subheading: _____

Topic sentence: _____

_____

Subheading: _____

Topic sentence: _____

_____

Subheading: _____

Topic sentence: _____

_____

Subheading: _____

Topic sentence: _____

_____

Subheading: _____

Topic sentence: _____

_____

Subheading: _____

Topic sentence: _____

_____

Using pronouns accurately

4 Insert the correct pronoun into each of these sentences.

a When Diego regained consciousness _____ was lying with his face in the snow.

b Javier and Diego had climbed together for years. _____ knew each other very well.

c Diego could hear the sound of running water. _____ made his throat feel even drier.

d Other climbers soon heard about the incident. _____ were not very forgiving.

Structuring paragraphs

5 Look again at these sentences from the first paragraph of the extract on page 242 of the Student Book:

A Fossils are the imprints of long-lost creatures, usually the hard parts of them such as bones, shells or teeth.

B But sometimes, as the mud in the ground or on the sea floor turns hard, the cells that make up their hard parts can be replaced by minerals, turning them to stone.

C Fossils are wonderful for helping scientists understand what kinds of creatures once lived on the Earth.

a Which is the topic sentence?

_____

b Which sentence(s) explain why fossils are useful?

_____

c Which sentence(s) give extra information about what fossils are?

_____

6 Look at the following facts and write a short paragraph with a topic sentence and supporting sentences giving additional information. You need not include all the facts.

- Armadillos have long claws which they use to dig for food: usually insects.
- Armadillos have short legs.
- Armadillos can move quickly.
- Armadillos roll up into a ball when threatened.
- Armadillos are armoured mammals native to the Americas.
- Armadillos have poor eyesight but a strong sense of smell.
- 'Armadillo' means 'little armoured one' in Spanish.

_____

_____

_____

_____

_____

_____

Set extension activity

7 Look again at your work in **Activity 3** on page 229 of this Workbook. Choose four of the subheadings and add a few sentences to the topic sentences you have already written to create four paragraphs. Each paragraph should include a topic sentence and some supporting sentences that give extra information or description.

Heading: **A guide to your new school**

Subheading: _____

_____

_____

_____

_____

_____

_____

Subheading: _____

_____

_____

_____

_____

_____

_____

Subheading: _____

_____

_____

_____

_____

_____

_____

Subheading: _____

_____

_____

_____

_____

_____

Section 8
Engaging the reader

In this section, you will practise exploring ways to entertain and engage your reader while you inform them.

Techniques for engaging the reader

1 Look again at the article on page 246 of the Student Book. Write down four examples of the writer using comparison to engage the reader.

_____

_____

_____

_____

2 How many times does the writer use statistics?

_____

3 What two things does the writer advise readers to do to protect their brains?

_____

_____

4 Reread this sentence from the article:

All the information and experiences you get from outside your body travels through that lump: everything you see, hear, smell, feel and taste; everything you think, and everything you do.

How does this sentence engage the reader with the topic of the brain? Write your answer below.

_____

_____

_____

5 How does the writer engage the reader in this article? Write a paragraph using quotations from the article.

_____

_____

_____

_____

Set extension activity

6 Pick a topic that you would not normally think of as interesting. Research your topic and write down ten surprising or interesting facts about it. You could choose one of the ideas below, or use your own idea.

bricks | water | bread | the tongue | ants

Using synonyms

7 Draw lines linking the pairs of words that are synonyms.

amazing	gradually
carefully	anxious
nervous	incredible
excited	cautiously
slowly	thrilled

8a Write down every synonym you can think of for the word 'loud'.

_____

_____

b Rewrite the following sentence, using the most appropriate synonym from those you identified in **Activity 8a**.

We heard a loud roar in the undergrowth.

Using engaging vocabulary

9a Place a tick next to the sentence below that is an example of sensory language.

A Nerves from your senses deliver information to your brain. ☐

B So it keeps your heart beating, your lungs breathing and your eyes blinking. ☐

C About twenty per cent of your body's energy is used up by your brain. ☐

b Rewrite the following sentence using more sensory language. (Tip: Hydrogen sulfide smells a bit like rotten eggs.)

The hot spring releases hydrogen sulfide into the air.

_____

_____

10 Rewrite the following sentences using more powerful vocabulary to engage the reader.

a The ear drum is really sensitive.

_____

_____

b The cheetah can run quickly. It is quicker than all other animals.

_____

_____

c The ground shook with a scary grumble as the earthquake hit. People ran out of the buildings.

_____

_____

Set extension activity

11a Look back at the facts you collected in **Activity 6** on page 233 of this Workbook. Write at least three paragraphs of an informative text on your chosen topic. Use powerful vocabulary and choose techniques that will engage the reader, such as:

- comparison
- explanation
- humour
- statistics
- advice.

b Look back over what you have written. Select three examples of powerful vocabulary that you have used and explain why you think they are effective.

This section links to pages 250–253 of the Student Book.

Section 9
Reaching conclusions

In this section, you will practise exploring ways in which you can begin and end information texts.

Proofreading full stops

1 Rewrite the following short paragraph, adding full stops and capital letters to punctuate it correctly.

at nearly 4,000 metres high, Mount Fuji is the biggest mountain in Japan it is also extremely busy – over 200,000 people climb 'Fuji-san' every year most people think that Mount Fuji is a volcano but not many realise that it is actually three volcanoes piled on top of one another don't worry though, it is not still active

_____

_____

_____

_____

_____

Text openings

2 Look again at the article on page 250 of the Student Book. The first paragraph is just one short sentence. How does this opening paragraph engage the reader? Explain your answer below.

_____

_____

_____

3a Write a similar short sentence to begin a biography about someone you are interested in. Try to make an instant impact on the reader.

_____

b Now write the second paragraph for your biography in no more than three sentences. Include some information about the person's childhood as well as describing at least one thing about them that is unusual or surprising.

_____

_____

_____

_____

_____

Set extension activity

4a Make some notes about the early years of your own life. Include the basic facts but also try to think of interesting, dramatic or unusual information that could be included in a biography. Think about:

- where you were born
- any stories you have heard about when you were a baby
- your earliest memories of playing with other children
- clothes and toys you remember
- adults and siblings in your life
- any accidents or trips to hospital
- a surprising fact about yourself/your life
- your proudest moment(s).

b Select three pieces of information that you could use in an opening paragraph to engage the reader. Which one would be most effective? Explain your answer below.

Structuring and planning a biography

5 You have been asked to create a guide for other people to follow when writing the biography of a famous person. Number these paragraphs from 1 to 4 to show the order that you think creates the right structure.

A A paragraph about their childhood.

B A paragraph including a strong statement about what the person achieved along with an interesting, unusual fact about them.

C A paragraph about how what they achieved had a lasting impact.

D A paragraph about the work they became famous for and their achievements.

6 You are going to plan a full biography of a famous person. You may wish to look back at the work you did for **Activity 3** on page 236 of this Workbook. Or you could choose a different famous person. Make notes detailing what you will include in four paragraphs following the structure you outlined in **Activity 5** above. Remember to include key pieces of information about your chosen person, as well as attention-grabbing, unusual facts.

Opening paragraph

_____

_____

_____

_____

Paragraph 2

_____

_____

_____

_____

Paragraph 3

_____

_____

_____

_____

Final paragraph

_____

_____

_____

_____

Set extension activity

7a Write the biography of a famous person that you planned in **Activity 6** on the previous page. Continue your answer in your notebook if needed. Remember to:

- follow your planned order
- include facts about your chosen person
- include interesting and dramatic information
- use short sentences for effect
- use capital letters and full stops correctly.

_____

_____

_____

_____

_____

_____

_____

_____

_____

_____

_____

_____

_____

_____

_____

_____

_____

_____

_____

_____

_____

_____

_____

b Look back over what you have written. Identify one thing that you have done particularly well and explain why it is effective.

_____

_____

_____

c Identify one thing you could change that would most significantly improve what you have written. Explain your answer below.

_____

_____

_____

Section 10
Planning a lesson

In this section, you will practise exploring ways of planning an informative speech.

A group of elderly people who have never used a computer before have asked you to make a presentation introducing computers and how to use them. You now need to prepare a lesson for them.

Gathering information

1 Note down five facts about computers that you think your audience will need to know, or find particularly interesting. Try to include several unusual or surprising facts.

The first computer was invented by a man called Doug Engelbart and was made out of wood!

A _____

B _____

C _____

D _____

E _____

Preparing to plan

2 Identify one fact that you think would be most effective in engaging your audience at the beginning of the presentation. Explain your choice below.

_____

_____

3a Note down the five things that you feel computers are most useful for.

A _____

B _____

C _____

D _____

E _____

b Which one of these points do you think your audience (elderly people who have never used computers) would most need to know about? Explain your answer below.

_____

_____

_____

Set extension activity

4 Making sure not to repeat any of the points you explored in **Activities 1** to **3**, choose one of the following headings:

- How to send an email
- How to search for something online
- How to use a word processor

a You are going to write a set of instructions explaining to your audience how to complete the 'How to' task you have chosen. Make some brief notes on the key steps you will need to explain.

_____

_____

_____

_____

_____

_____

b Write a clear set of instructions explaining how to do it. Continue in your notebook if needed. Remember to:

- use a numbered list
- use imperative verbs and the correct person and tense (see page 234 of the Student Book to remind yourself how to do this)
- include everything your audience needs to know, and nothing they do not need to know.

_____

_____

_____

_____

_____

_____

_____

_____

c Write a final paragraph explaining how the audience will benefit now that they have learned this skill.

_____

_____

_____

_____

_____

Sequencing

5a What sort of topics are best suited to texts presented in chronological order? Explain your answer below.

_____

_____

_____

b What sort of topics should be presented as step-by-step instructions? Explain your answer below.

_____

_____

_____

c What sort of topics are best suited to texts presented as paragraphs that cover different aspects of the topic? Explain your answer below.

_____

_____

_____

6a Look at the work you did on page 240 of this Workbook, gathering facts for a presentation about using computers. What subheadings might you use to structure your presentation? For example: _How computers affect the world; What computers can be used for._
Note down three subheadings and note two or three points beneath each one.

Subheading: _____ ☐

_____

_____

Subheading: _____ ☐

_____

_____

Subheading: _____ ☐

_____

_____

b In the boxes next to the subheadings, write numbers to indicate the order in which they would be structured in your presentation.

Set extension activity

7 Revise the skills you have covered in the second half of this unit, ready for the assessment in the next lesson. You may find it helpful to note down the key points covered in each of the sections so far. If there are any areas where you do not feel confident, reread the appropriate pages in the Student Book. Think back to when you planned for the previous assessment. What helped? What could you improve on?

Section 7: Paragraphing information

A topic sentence sums up the rest of the information in a paragraph.

Section 8: Engaging the reader

Section 9: Reaching conclusions

Section 10: Planning a lesson

This section links to pages 258–259 of the Student Book.

Section 11
Assessment

In this section, you will identify the mistakes in a sample student response and write an improved version.

1 Look at the following task and read the student's response that follows.

> **Task:** Write the text for a short presentation introducing bicycles and how to use them to people who have never seen a bicycle before.

> **Response:** You rode a bike by pedal and if you want to stop then people squeezed the break but there are two breaks, one for each wheel so to steer they can turning the handle bars. It can be difficult to balance and there is lots of different types of bikes and some people raced them in competions because bikes are fun to ride.
> Bikes have been invented arond 200 years ago. Bikes are very effishent. Bikes are very cheep to make compaired to cars. Bikes are very good for the environment. Bikes are cheep to look after. Bikes last a long time. Bikes were used all over the world. Peple used bikes for fun and to get around.

You are going to improve and extend this response.

a Underline any spelling or punctuation mistakes.
b Circle any verbs that are in the wrong tense.
c Write a 'V' next to any opportunities to improve the impact of the writing by making different vocabulary choices.
d Write an 'S' next to any opportunities to improve the impact of the writing by varying sentence length and structure.
e Use the space in the box below to make some notes and plan how you will improve and extend this answer.

2 Write your improved version of the answer in the space below. Remember to include:

- clear directions explaining how to use a bicycle
- appropriate structural features such as bulleted or numbered lists
- direct address and imperative verbs
- an introduction
- a final safety warning.

Notes

Published by Pearson Education Limited, 80 Strand, London, WC2R 0RL.

www.pearsonglobalschools.com

Text © Pearson Education Limited 2020
Designed by Pearson Education Limited 2020
Typeset by SPi Global
Edited by Judith John, Liliane Nénot and Judith Shaw
Original illustrations © Pearson Education Limited 2020
Cover design © Pearson Education Limited 2020
With thanks to Stephen Cunningham

Cover images: *Front:* Getty Images/Santiago Urquijo

The right of Ben Hulme-Cross to be identified as the author of this work has been asserted by him in accordance with the Copyright, Designs and Patents Act 1988.

First published 2020

25
10 9 8

British Library Cataloguing in Publication Data
A catalogue record for this book is available from the British Library

ISBN 978 0 435 20078 7

Printed in Slovakia by Neografia